Burford Ontario Book 2 and Area in Colour Photos, Saving Our History One Photo at a Time

Photography
by Barbara Raué
2017

Series Name:
Cruising Ontario

Book 183: Burford Book 2 and Area

Cover photo: 374 Maple Avenue South, Page 14

Series Name: Cruising Ontario
Saving Our History One Photo at a Time
in colour photos

Books Available in Alphabetical Order:
Aberfoyle, Acton, Alton, Amherstburg, Ancaster, Arthur, Aylmer, Ayr, Bloomingdale, Brantford, Burlington, Caledon, Caledonia, Cambridge, Clifford, Conestogo, Delhi, Dorchester to Aylmer, Drayton, Drumbo, Dundas, Eden Mills, Elmira, Elora, Essex, Fergus, Guelph, Hagersville, Hamilton, Hanover, Harriston, Hespeler, Jarvis, Kingston, Kingsville, Kitchener, Linwood, Listowel, London, Lucknow, Mono, Mount Forest, Neustadt, New Hamburg, Niagara-on-the-Lake, Oakville, Orangeville, Orillia, Owen Sound, Palmerston, Peterborough, Petrolia, Port Elgin, Preston, Rockwood, Sarnia, Seaforth, Sheffield, Shelburne, Simcoe, Southampton, St. Jacobs, St. Marys, St. Thomas, Stoney Creek, Stratford, Thamesford, Tillsonburg, Waterdown, Waterford, Waterloo, Welland, Wellesley, Windsor, Wingham, Woodstock

Book 157: Brockville
Book 158: Merrickville
Book 159: Smiths Falls
Book 160: Portland, Newboro
Book 161: Westport & Area
Book 162: Perth
Book 163-166: Belleville
Book 167-168: Port Colborne
Book 169: Erin in Colour
Book 170: Goderich in Colour
Book 171: Sault Ste. Marie
Book 172: Lake Superior
Book 173-176: Thunder Bay
Book 177-179: Paris

Book 180: St. George
Book 182-183: Burford

Other Books by Barbara Raue

Coins of Gold

Arrows, Indians and Love

The Life and Times of Barbara
Volume 1: Inventions That Have Enhanced My Life
Volume 2: Entertainment That I Have Enjoyed
Volume 3: East Coast Trips
Volume 4: Olympics Have Always Intrigued Me
Volume 5: Wonders of the World
Volume 6: Caribbean Cruises We Have Enjoyed
Volume 7: Animals
Volume 8: Storms and Other Major Disasters in My Lifetime
Volume 9: Wars, Terrorist Attacks and Major Disasters

The Cromwell Family Book

Laura Secord Discovered

Daddy Where Are You?

Montana Series
Book 1: Montana Dream
Book 2: Life on the Montana Frontier
Book 3: Montana to Boston and Back
Book 4: Montana Sons Go to War
Book 5: Montana Sons Return From War

Visit Barbara's website to view all of her books
http://barbararaue.ca

Table of Contents

Burford
      Maple Avenue South   Page 8

      Fairfield Road   Page 25

      Bishopsgate Road   Page 27

Mount Vernon   Page 34
    Highway 53
    Colborne Street West

Bishopsgate   Page 38

Langford   Page 39
    Colborne Street East

Burtch   Page 41

Architectural Terms   Page 42

Building Styles   Page 45

Burford is in the County of Brant and is located eight kilometers west of the City of Brantford along Highway 53, and seventy kilometers east of London.

In 1793 Lieutenant-Governor Simcoe granted to Abraham Dayton the entire Township of Burford. Dayton was a native of Milford, Connecticut. The township was to become the "new Jerusalem" for a religious sect with which he was affiliated. Dayton broke his ties with the sect and settled just west of the present village of Burford. He was responsible for bringing several families into the township and by the spring of 1797 the new settlement consisted of twenty-one families. Abraham Dayton died March 1, 1797 after a prolonged illness. Abigail Dayton, Abraham's widow, later married Colonel Joel Stone and moved to Gananoque where she lived until her death in 1843 at the age of 93. The Dayton's only child, Abiah, was the wife of Benajah Mallory and she and her husband followed her parents into this township. Benajah Mallory became a man of considerable influence and by 1805 was elected Member of the Legislative Assembly of Upper Canada representing Norfolk, Oxford, and Middlesex. In June 1812, war was declared against Upper Canada by the United States. During the course of the war, Mallory accepted a commission in the U.S. forces and was considered a traitor back home. Benajah Mallory became outlawed and his land was forfeited to the Crown.

John Yeigh, his wife Mary and their children Jacob, John Junior, Adam, Henry and Eva arrived in Burford from Pennsylvania by covered wagon in June 1800. The family cleared land, farmed and established the first pottery in the Burford area. Jacob and Adam distinguished themselves in the War of 1812 and were also active participants in the 1837 Rebellion.

Mount Vernon was originally named Springfield and subsequently Chequered Sheds because the posts were painted in black and white checkerboard fashion to mark several parking spots for rigs at the hotel across from Kenny's Store. The present name, according to oral history, was given by a railway company in honor of the home of George Washington, the first president of the United States.

Thomas Perrin laid out the village. He established the first store in 1835, built the first sawmill in 1840 and the first gristmill in 1845.

Bishopsgate is located on Highway 53 between Mount Vernon and Burford.

Langford is located on Highway 2/53 east of Fairchild's Creek about three kilometres east of Cainsville. The village was named for Jacob Lang, an early settler who came from Pennsylvania to this area about 1807. United Empire Loyalists settled here in the late 1700s. Several streams flowing south gave power to saw and grist mills in the area. A brickyard and a blacksmith shop were established here. The first post office was called Lang's Ford as all of the travelers had to ford the swampy stream in the hollow just east of Jacob Lang's farm. Later the name was changed to Langford.

Burtch was named for pioneer Stephen Burtch who owned farmland from Burtch to Mount Pleasant. A general store, wagon factory, and a blacksmith shop served the residents.

During World War II, Number 4 Wireless School, R.C.A.F. was located near the corner of Cockshutt and Burtch Roads. After the war, the base was converted to Burtch Industrial Farm. Fruits and vegetables were grown and much of the crop was processed at the cannery on site. Livestock was also raised here for meat. Farming ceased and the site was converted to the Burtch Correctional Centre in 1948 and inmates did volunteer work with the community. It operated until January 2003.

On February 28, 2006 the Six Nations of the Grand River began a demonstration at the Caledonia housing development to protest a land claim near Caledonia. The government offered them the 153-hectare Burtch site as part of a $125 million settlement for three land claims. The Six Nations wanted the Burtch facility to be demolished and reverted back to land. The cost of decommissioning and demolishing the site was reported to be $1 million. At the time there were thirty-seven buildings on the site. In 2008 a First Nations development company wanted to transform the center into an aboriginal healing and rehabilitation facility.

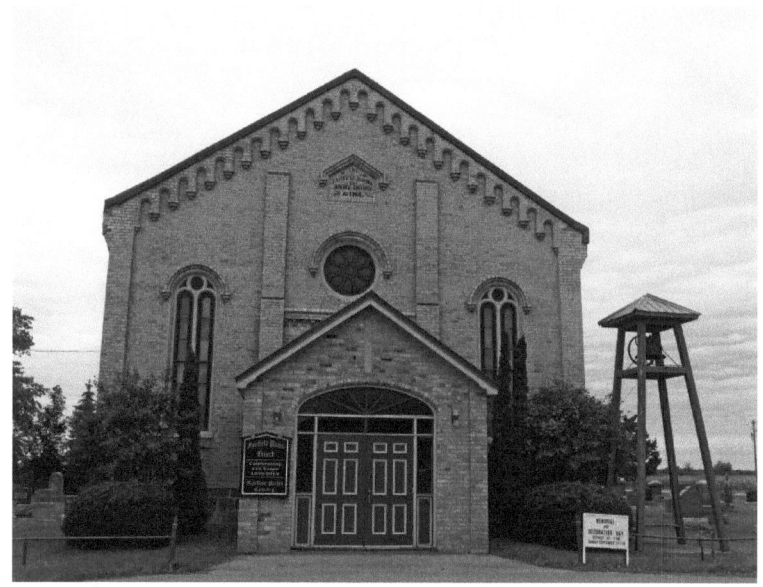

187 Maple Avenue South – Fairfield Plains United Church – A. D. 1868 – Italianate brickwork with the brick under the gable ends in "swags" and hooded Roman arched windows with stained glass, rose window, stone foundation

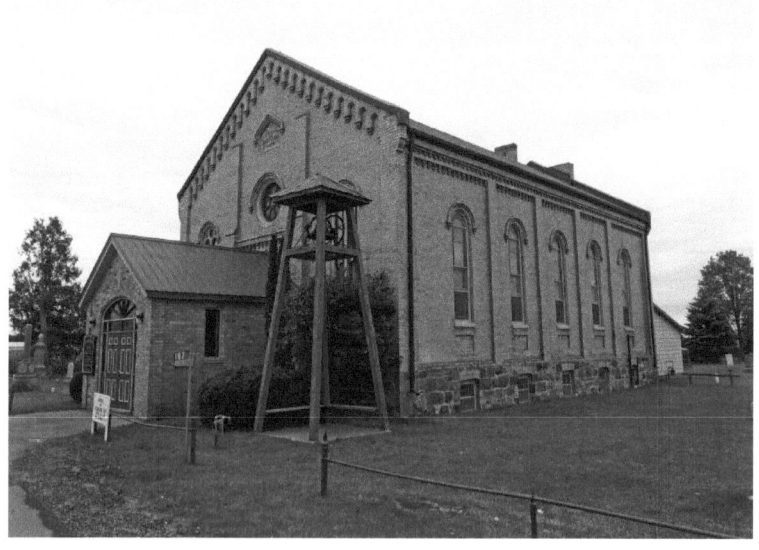

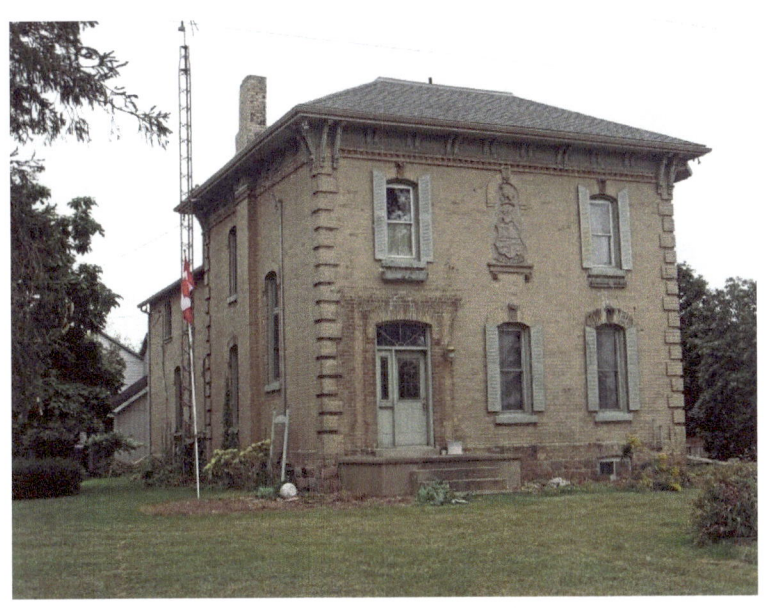

280 Maple Avenue South – built in Neo-Classical style by W. H. Metcalf - hipped roof, cornice brackets, raised corner quoins

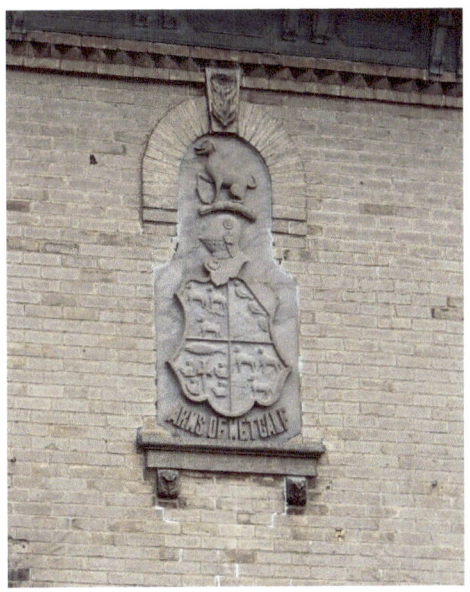

Metcalf Family Crest

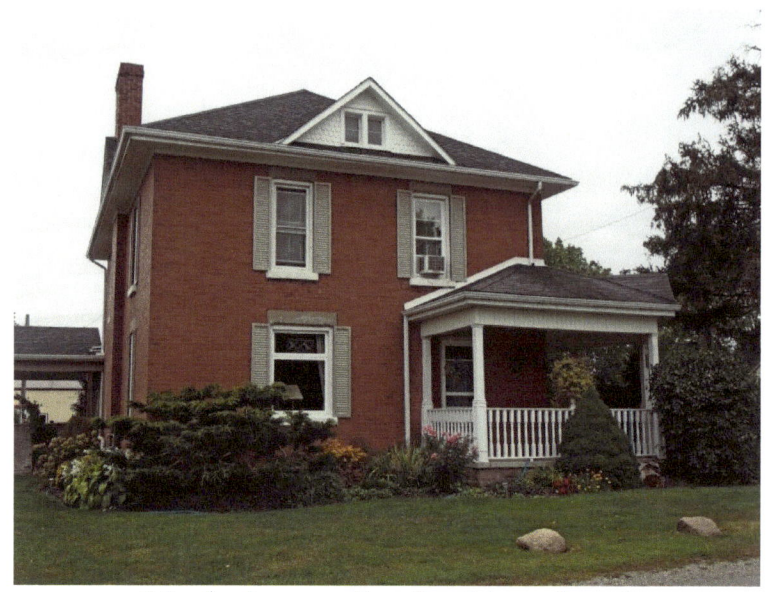

Maple Avenue South – hipped roof

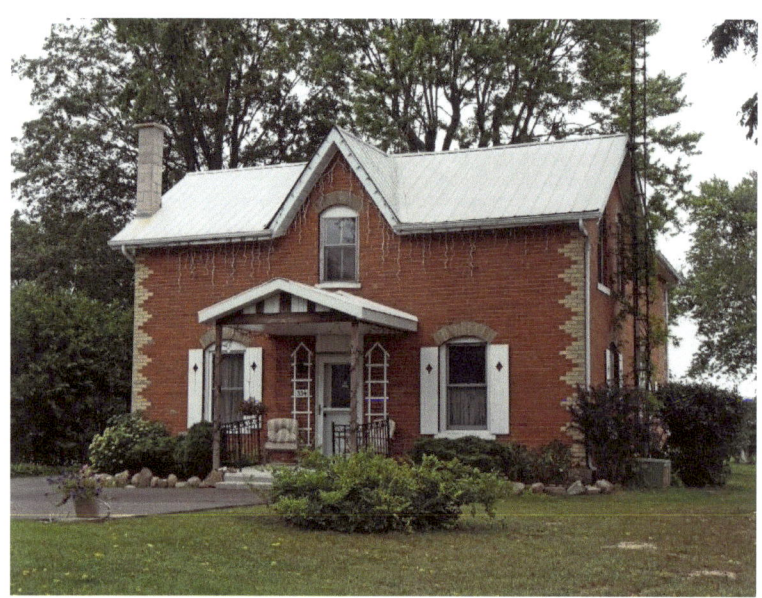

354 Maple Avenue South – Gothic – dichromatic brickwork on corners

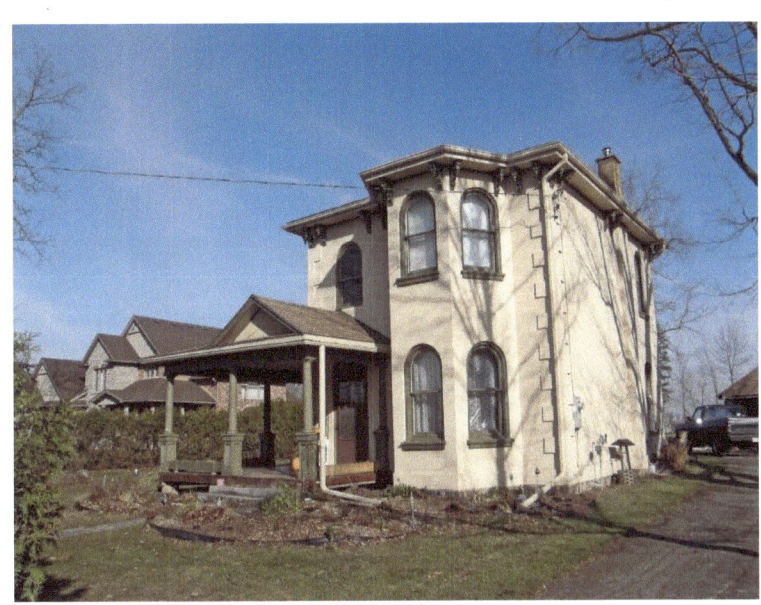

Maple Avenue South – Italianate - two-storey bay window, cornice brackets, corner quoins, pediment

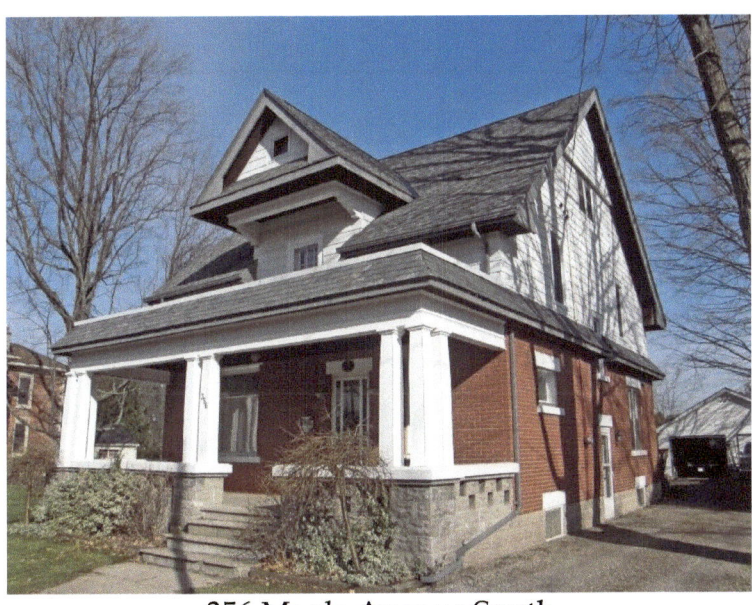

356 Maple Avenue South

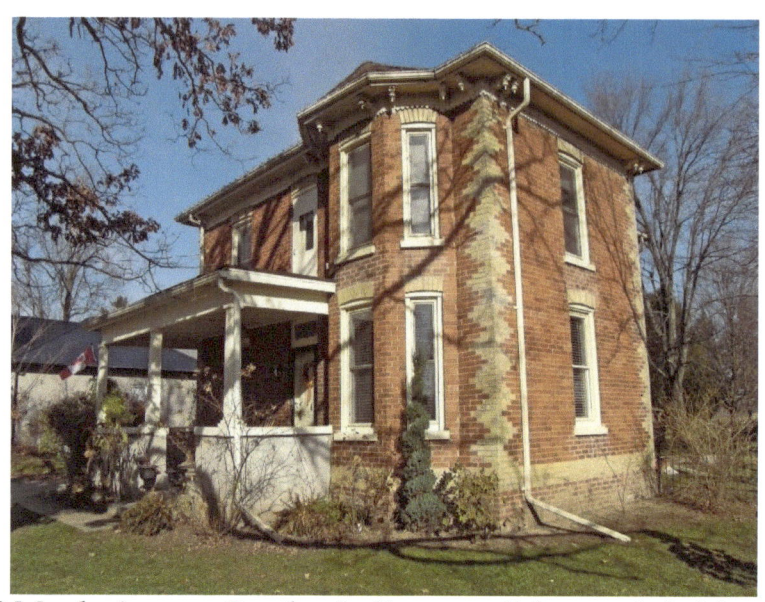

358 Maple Avenue South – Italianate - dichromatic brickwork on corners

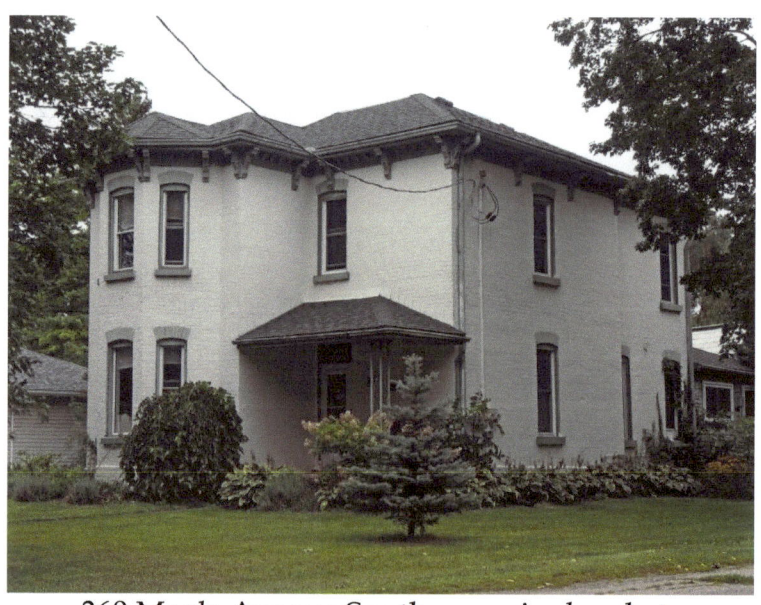

360 Maple Avenue South – cornice brackets

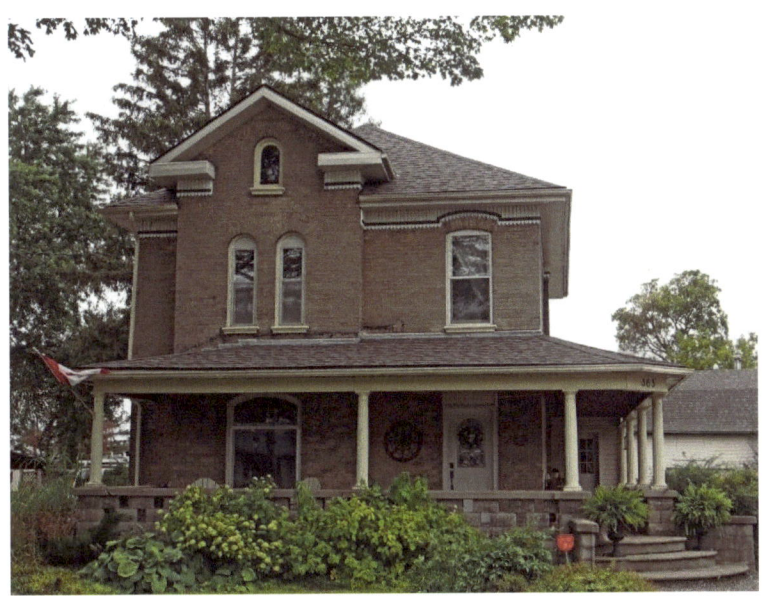

363 Maple Avenue South – built in the Queen Anne style by George Holt with a wraparound porch with wooden pillars. The upper storey has a bay window with one gable and cornice returns and rounded windows. There is decorative fretting under the eaves.

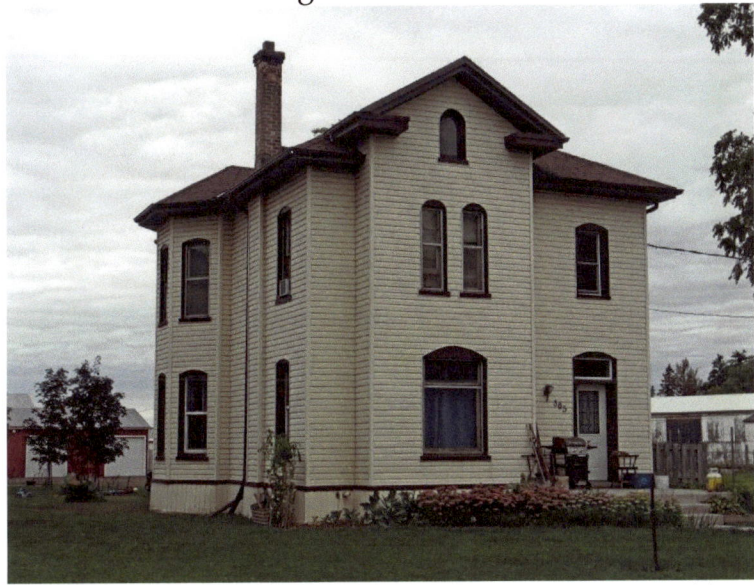

365 Maple Avenue South – cornice return on gable

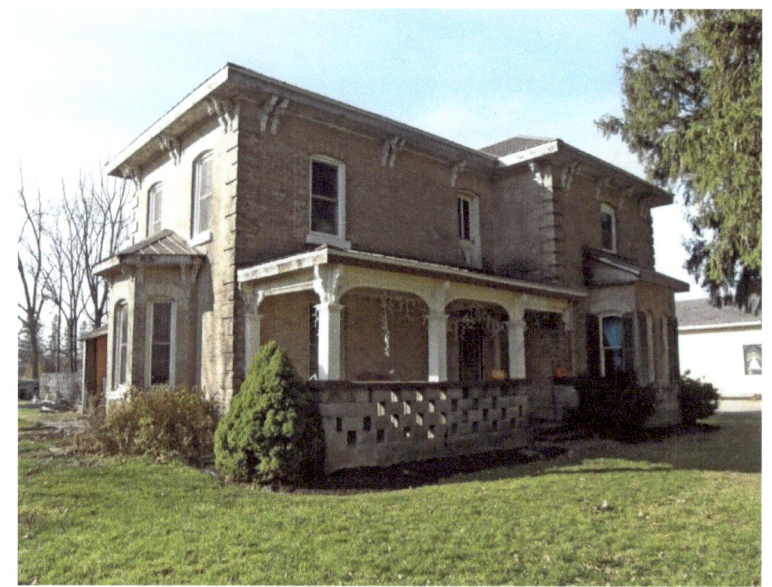

371 Maple Avenue South – paired cornice brackets, corner quoins

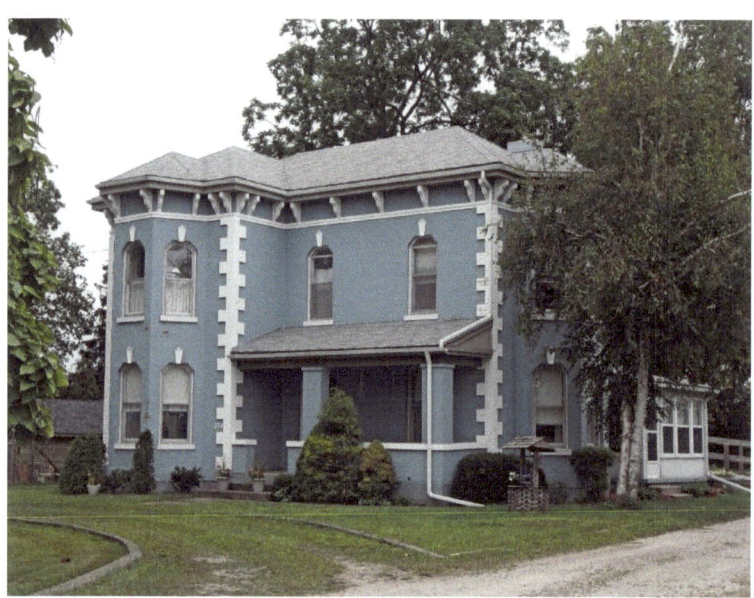

374 Maple Avenue South – cornice brackets, corner quoins

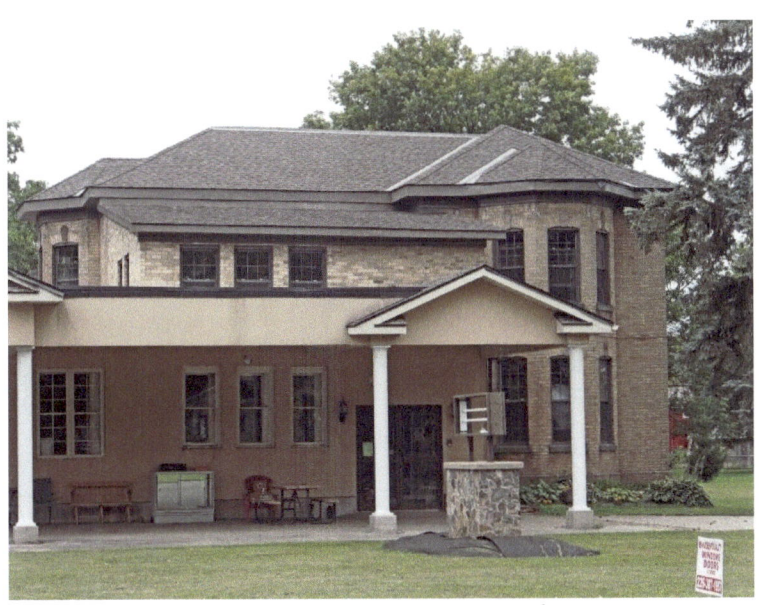

375 Maple Avenue South

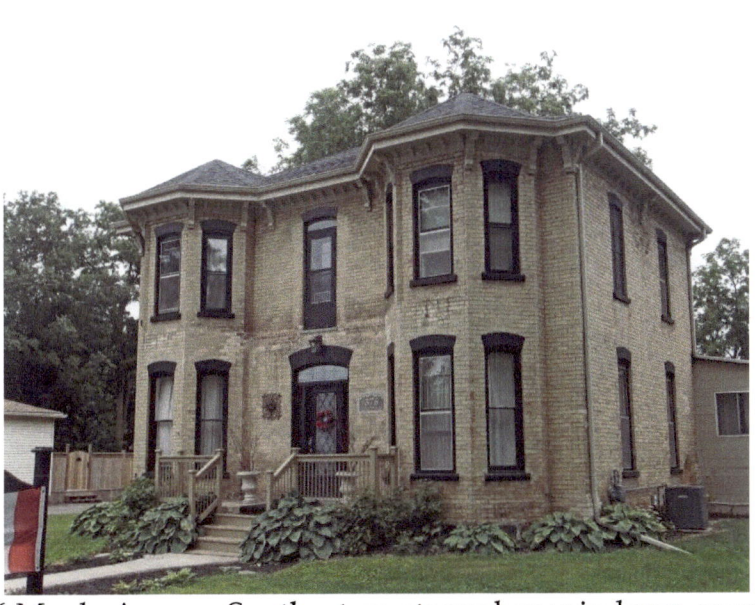

376 Maple Avenue South – two-storey bay windows, cornice brackets

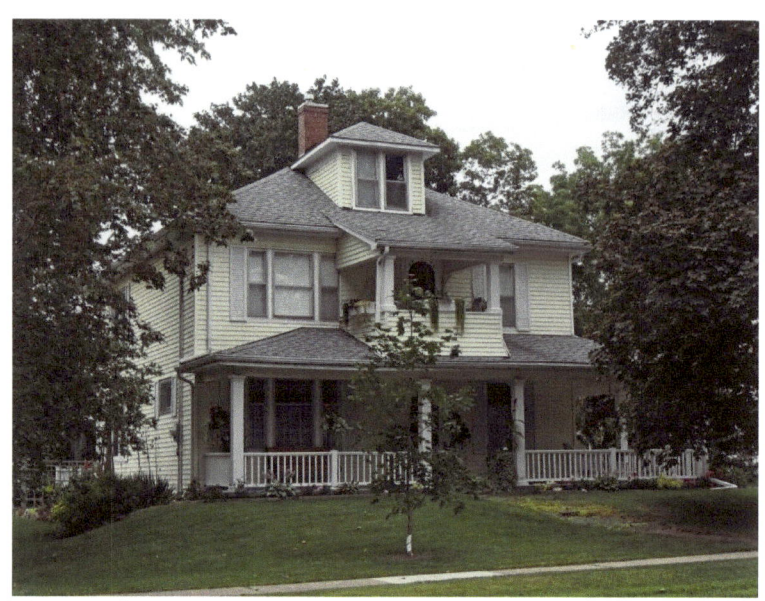

381 Maple Avenue South – dormer in roof, second floor veranda

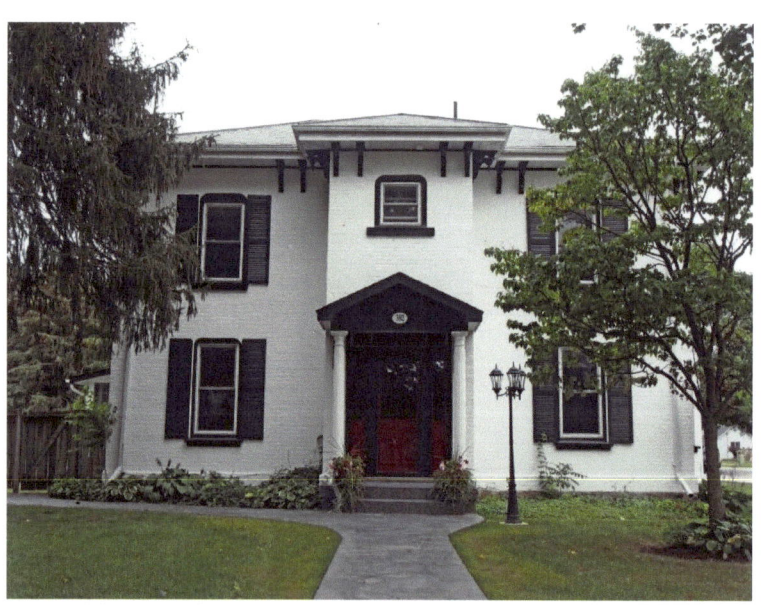

382 Maple Avenue South – cornice brackets

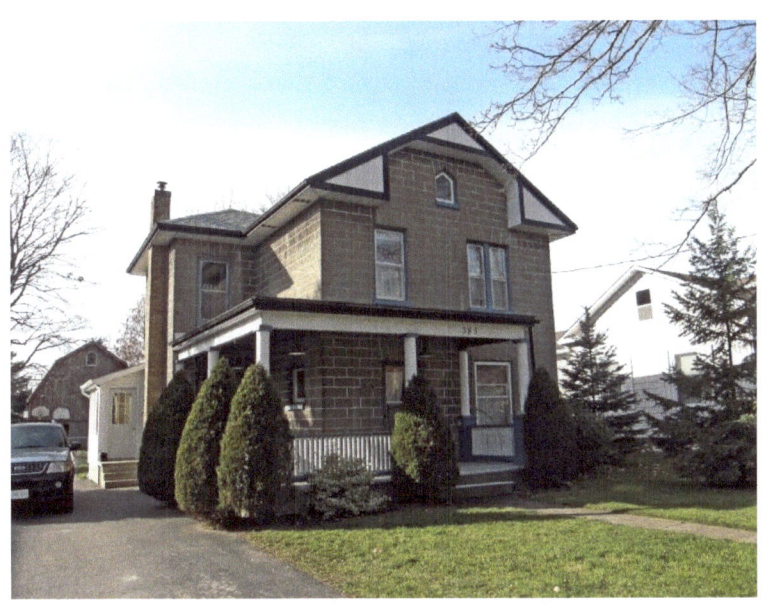

383 Maple Avenue South

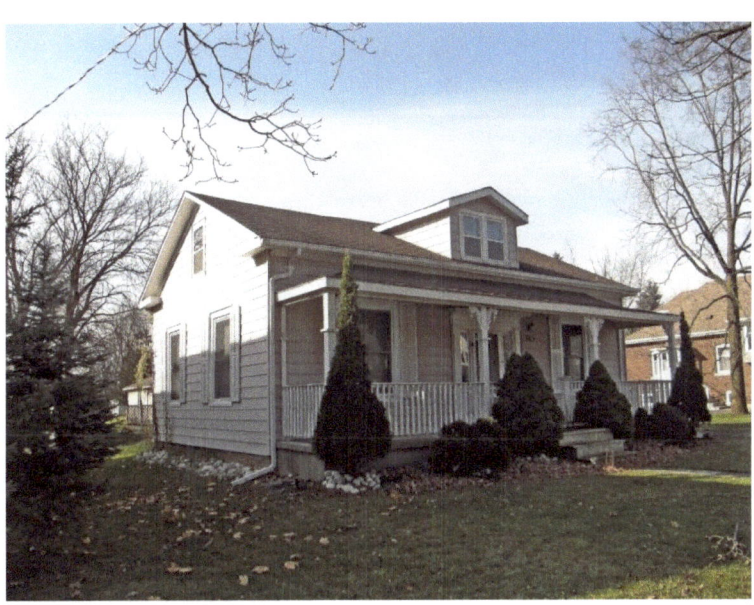

385 Maple Avenue South – dormer, cornice return on gable

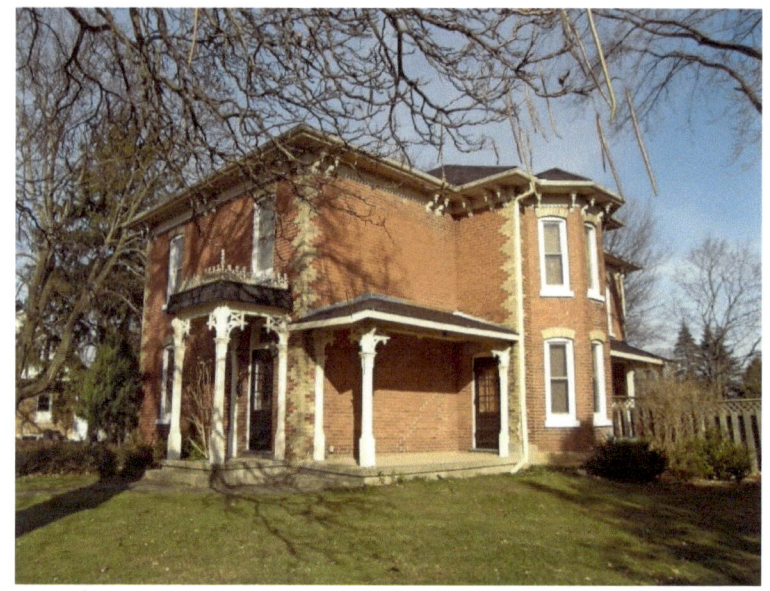

386 Maple Avenue South – dichromatic brickwork on corners, iron cresting above porch, two-storey bay window, brackets

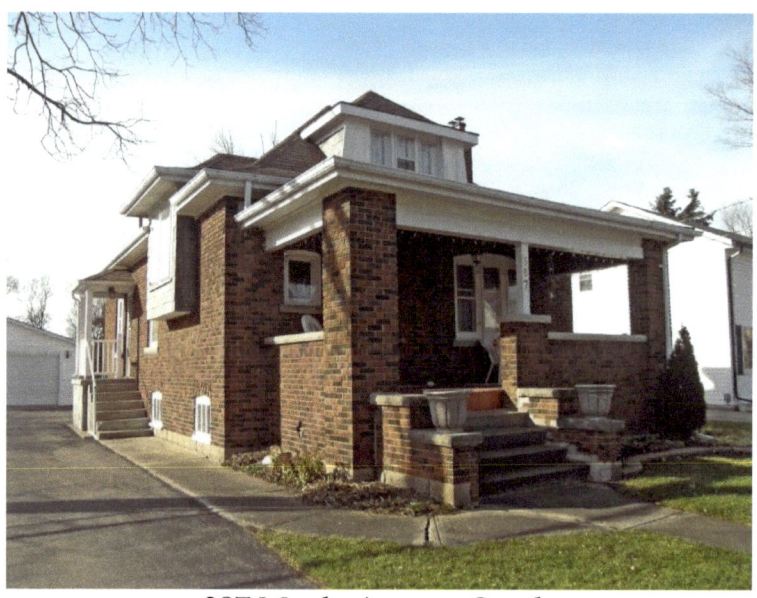

387 Maple Avenue South

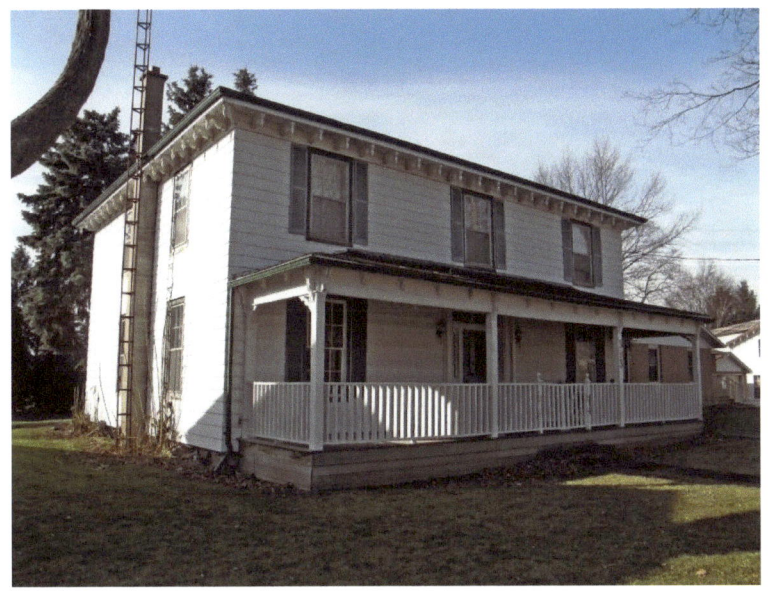

393 Maple Avenue South

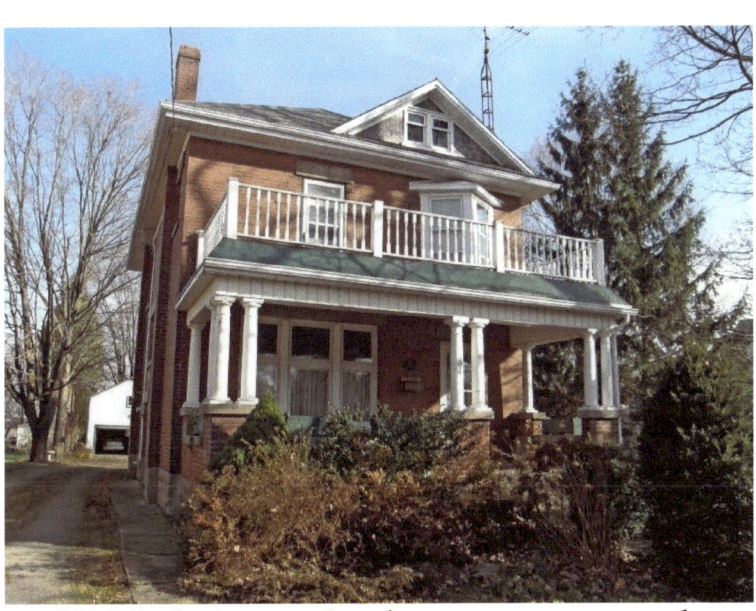

394 Maple Avenue South – two-storey veranda

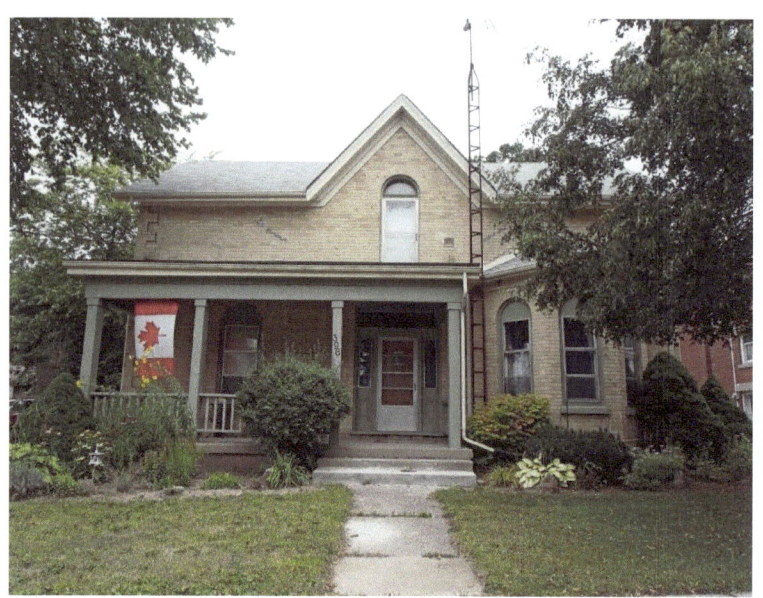

396 Maple Avenue South – bay window

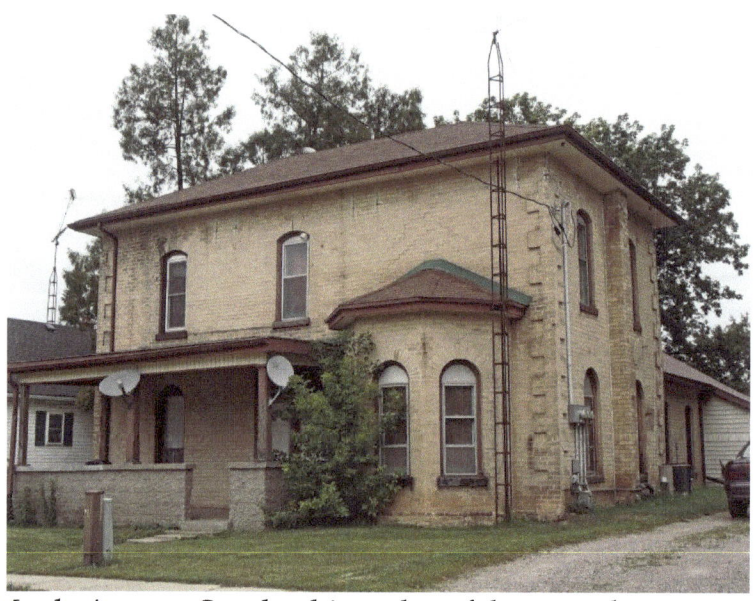

Maple Avenue South – hipped roof, bay window, corner quoins

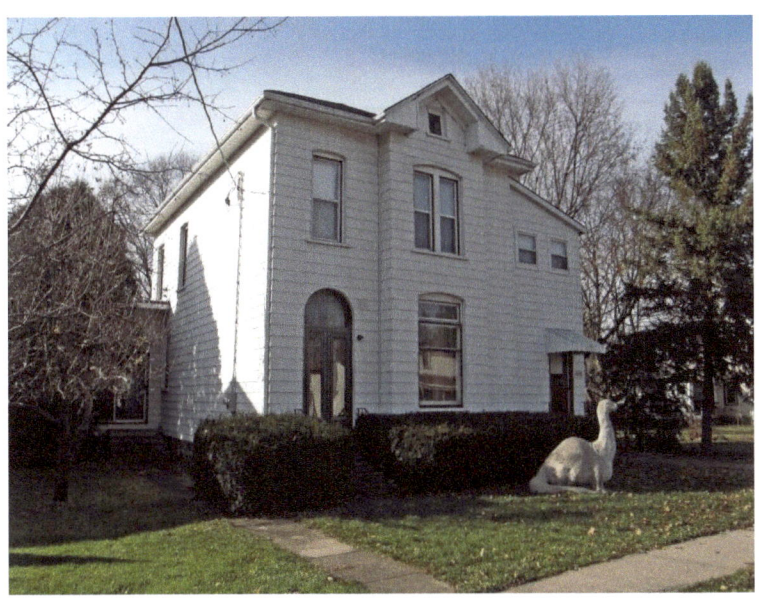

401 Maple Avenue South – 2½-storey frontispiece

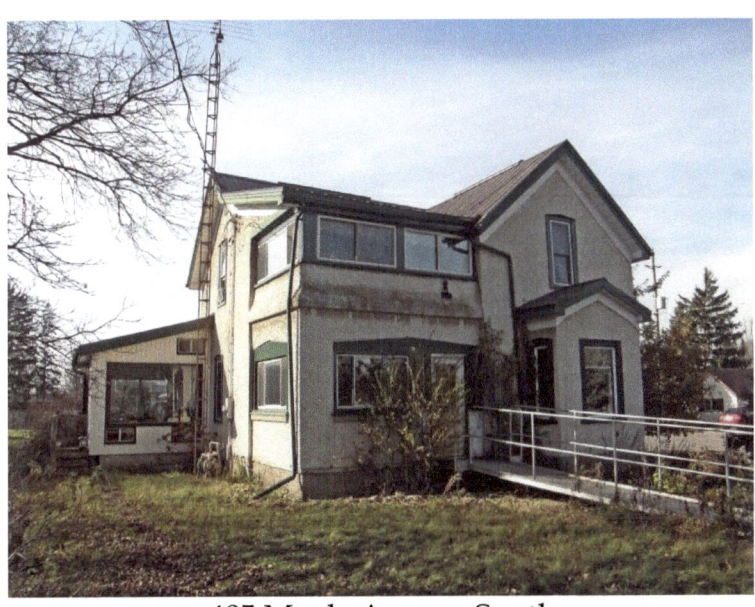

405 Maple Avenue South

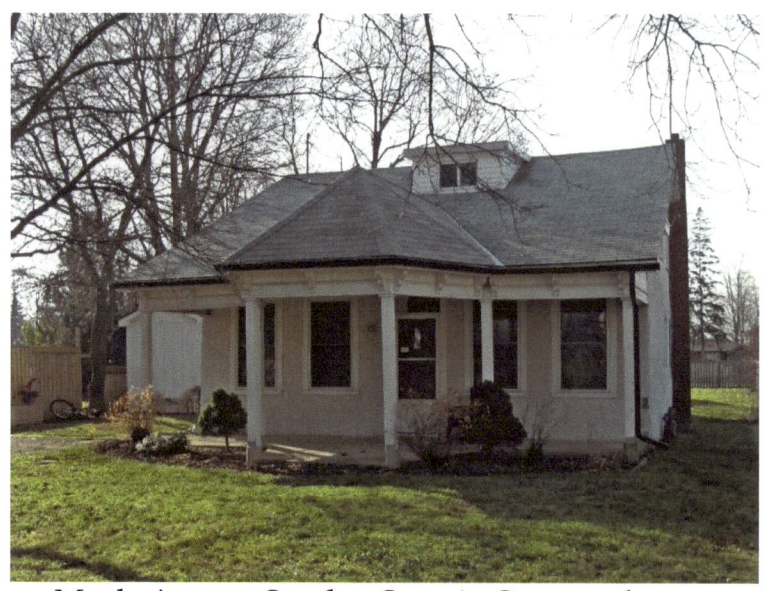
Maple Avenue South – Ontario Cottage, dormer

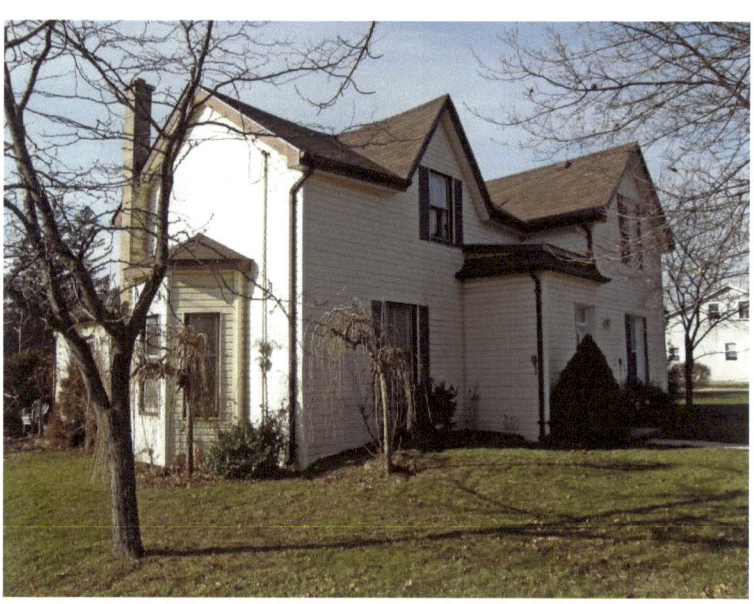
Maple Avenue South - Gothic

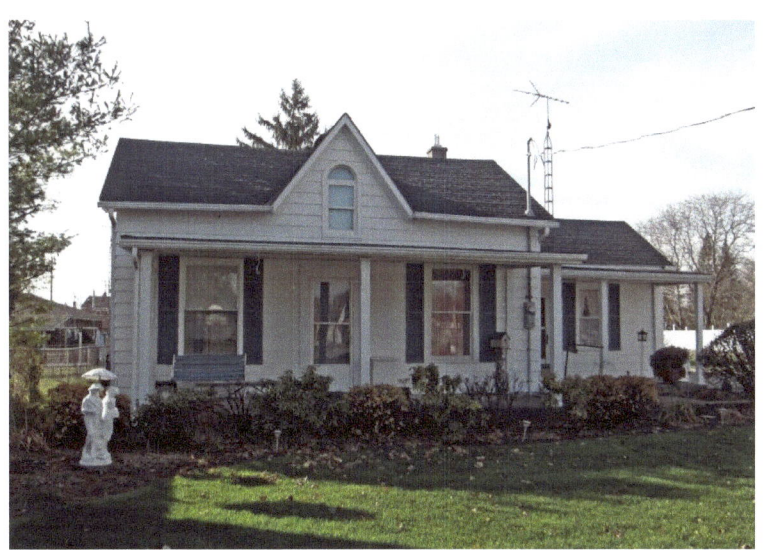

Maple Avenue South - Gothic

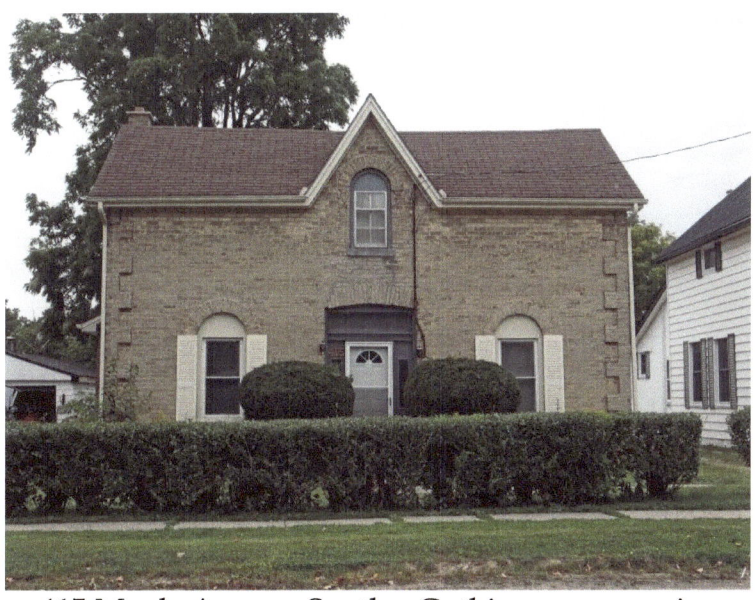

415 Maple Avenue South – Gothic, corner quoins

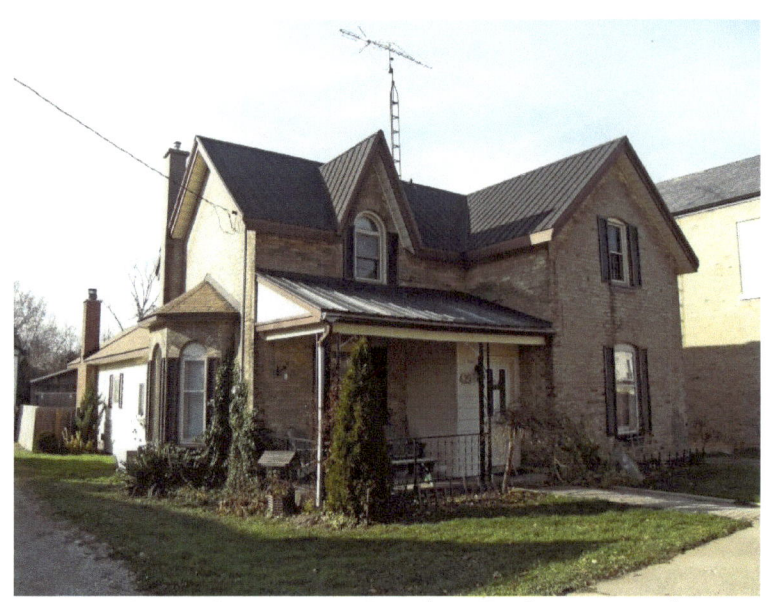

419 Maple Avenue South – Gothic Revival

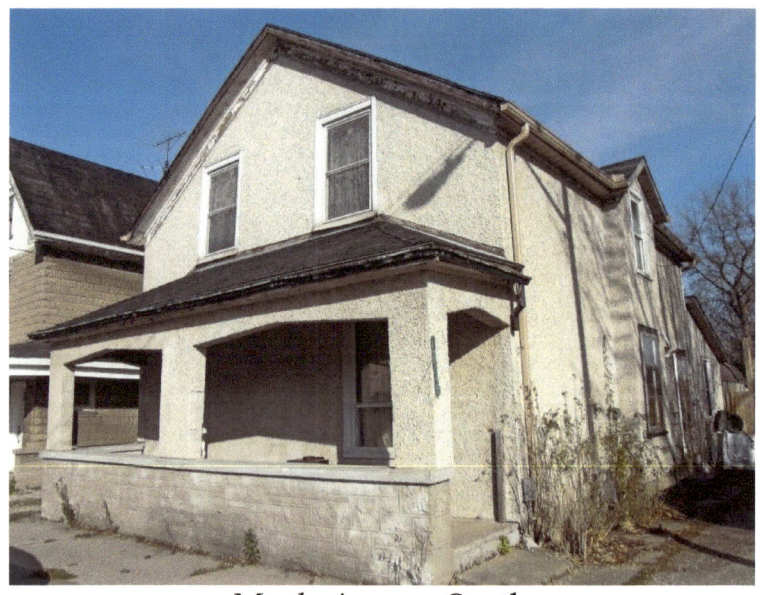

Maple Avenue South

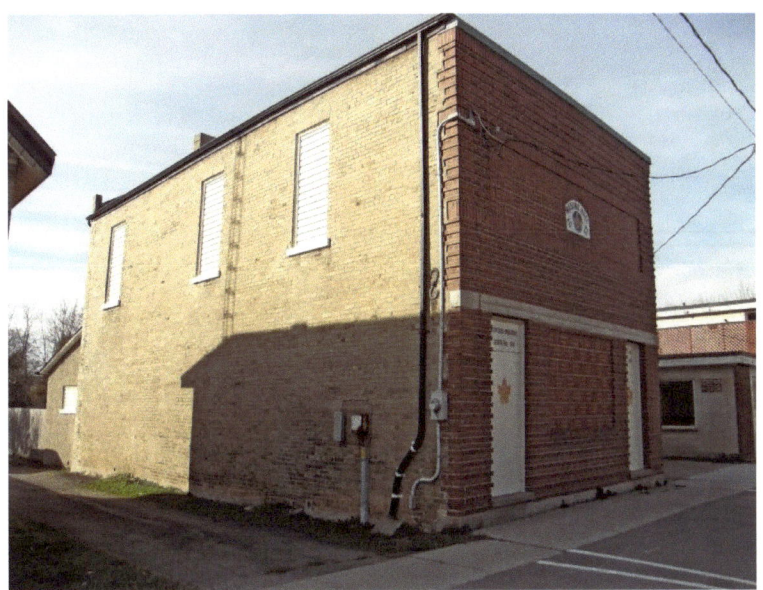

421 Maple Avenue South – Masonic Hall – 1883

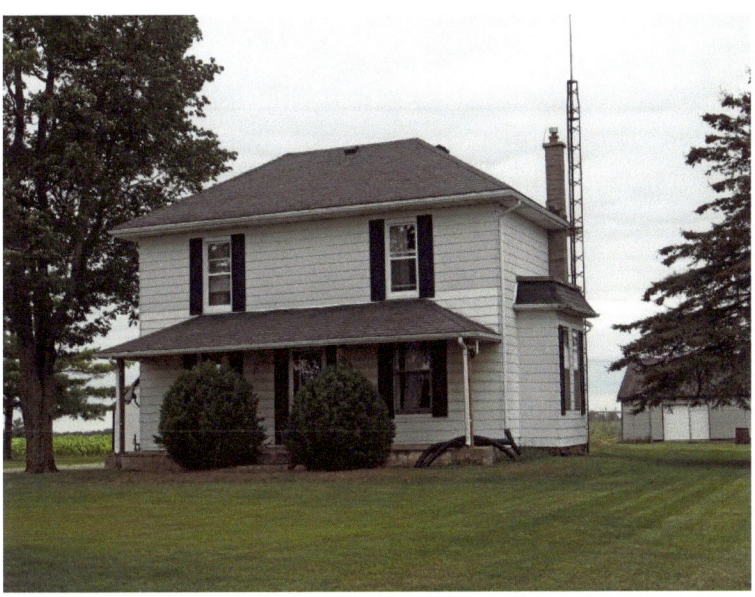

84 Fairfield Road – hipped roof

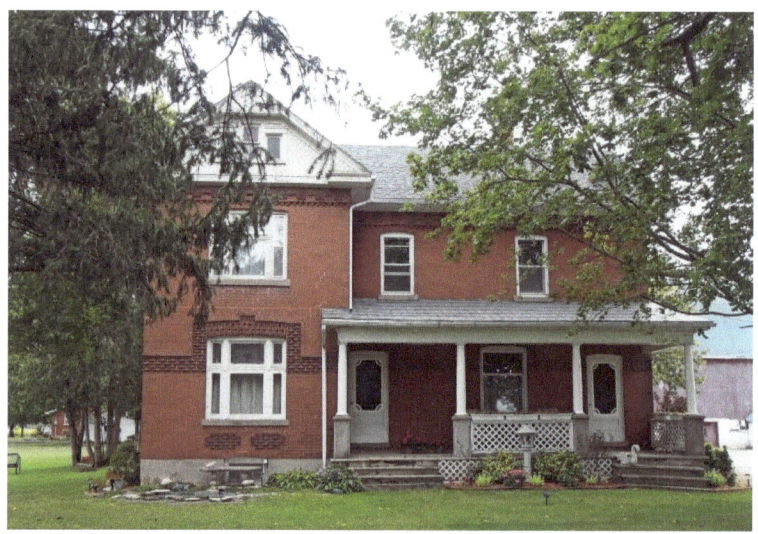

114 Fairfield Road – 1891 – Jacob Williams built this house of red brick with a slate roof, beautiful stained glass windows and decorative brickwork over and under the windows. Front and side porches are original.

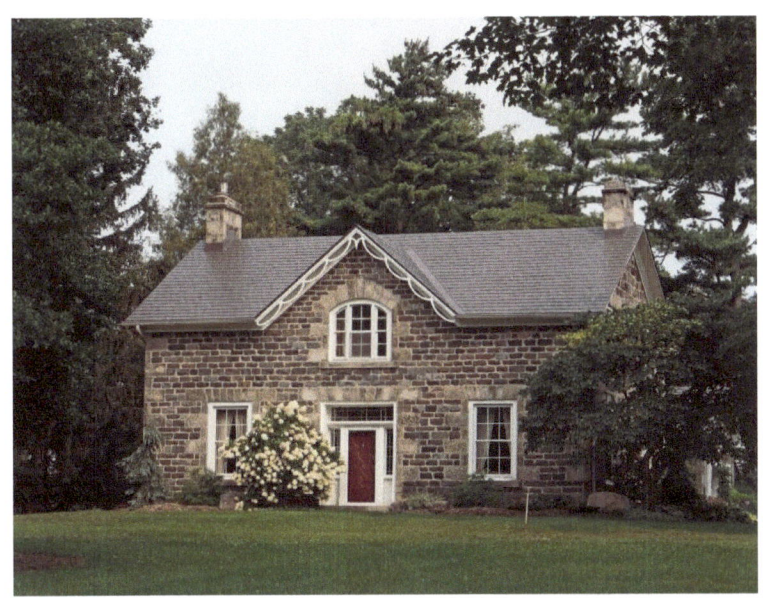

193 Bishopsgate Road – Gothic – verge board trim on gable

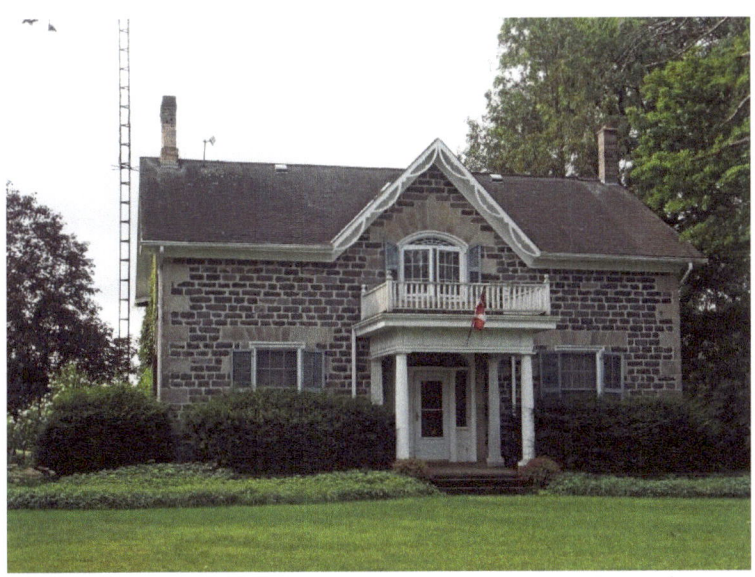

212 Bishopsgate Road – corner quoins, verge board trim on gable, second floor balcony

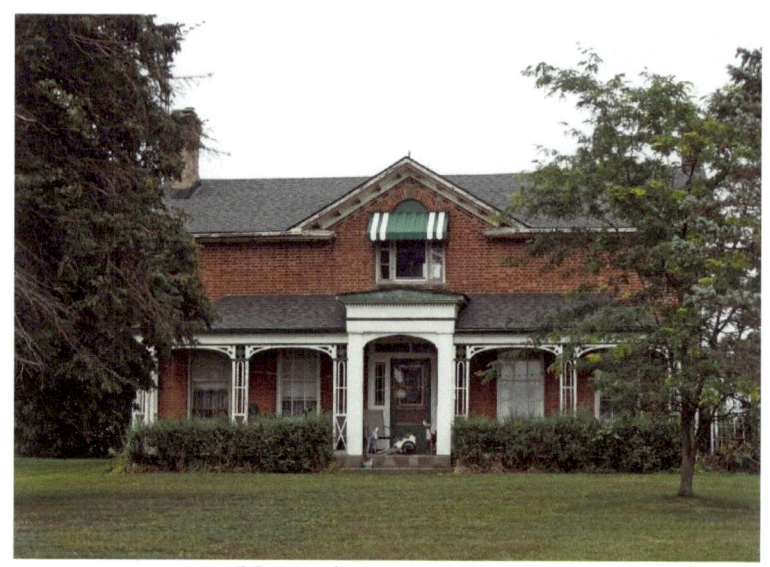
224 Bishopsgate Road

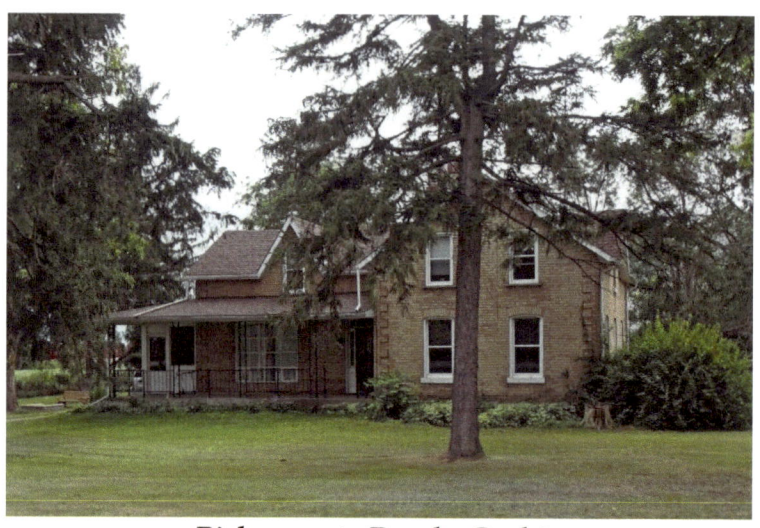
Bishopsgate Road - Gothic

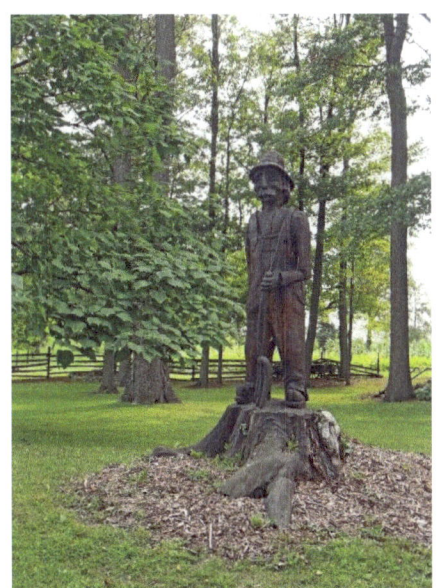

Carving

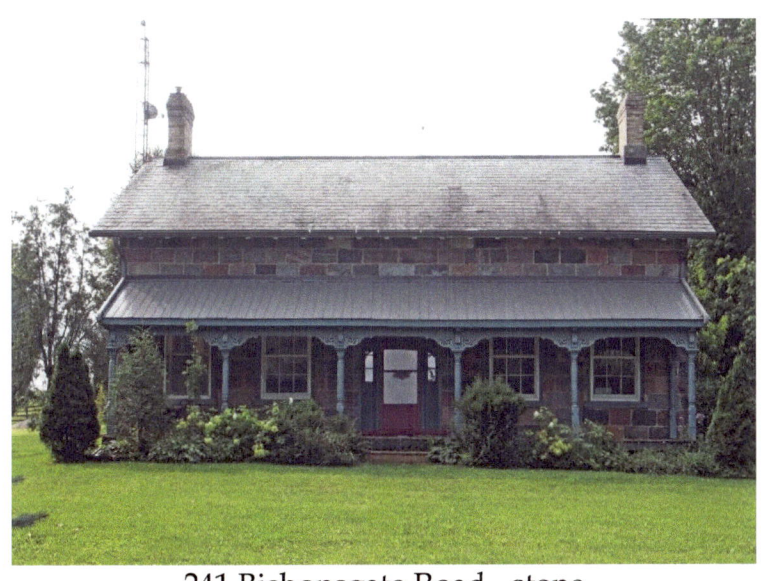

241 Bishopsgate Road - stone

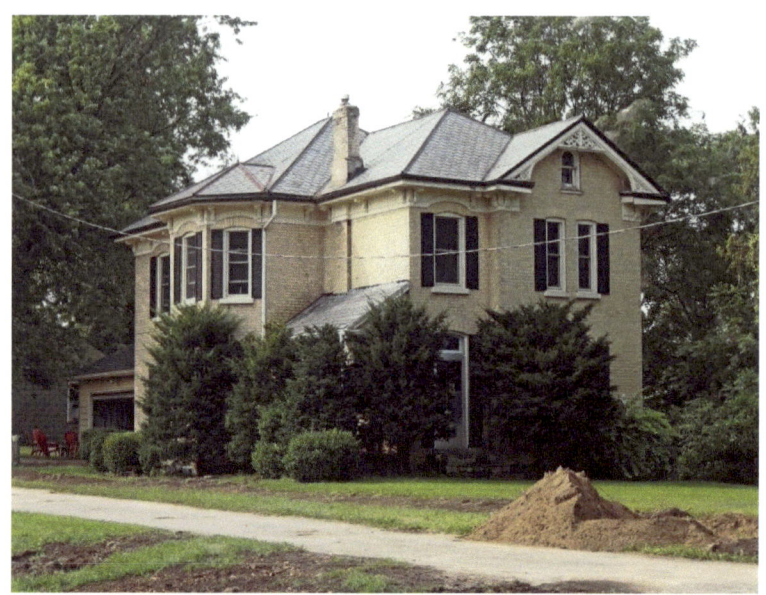

266 Bishopsgate Road – Queen Anne style – verge board trim on gable, cornice brackets

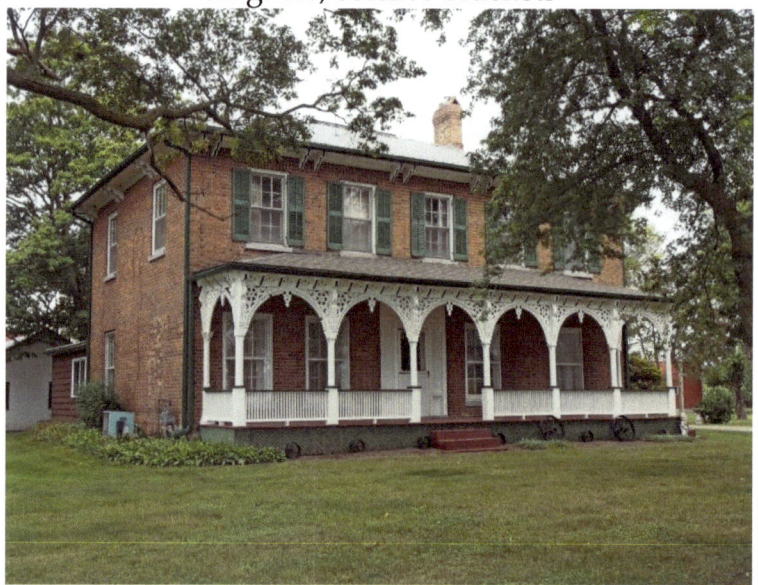

270 Bishopsgate Road – This Georgian house has elaborate porch arches and gingerbread with intricate fretwork. The windows are six over six panes.

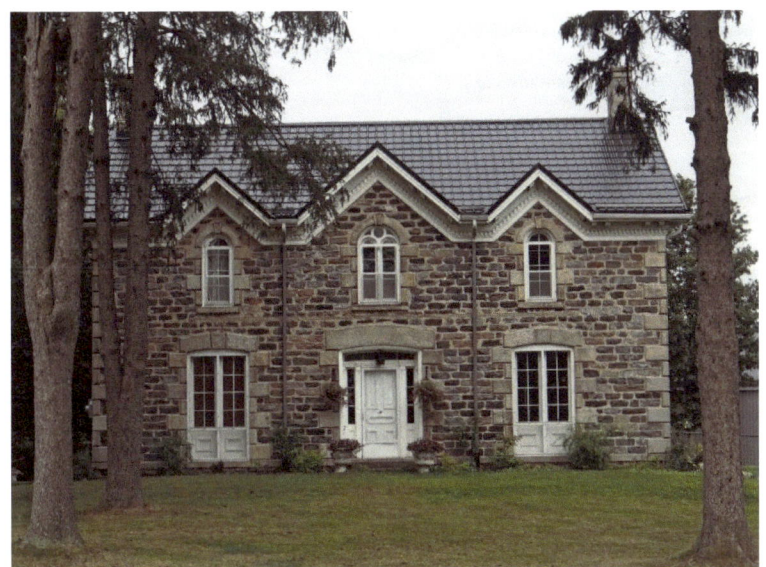

300 Bishopsgate Road – 1860 – This house has a beautiful field stone façade with extensive use of finely dressed limestone quoins, lintels and window labels.

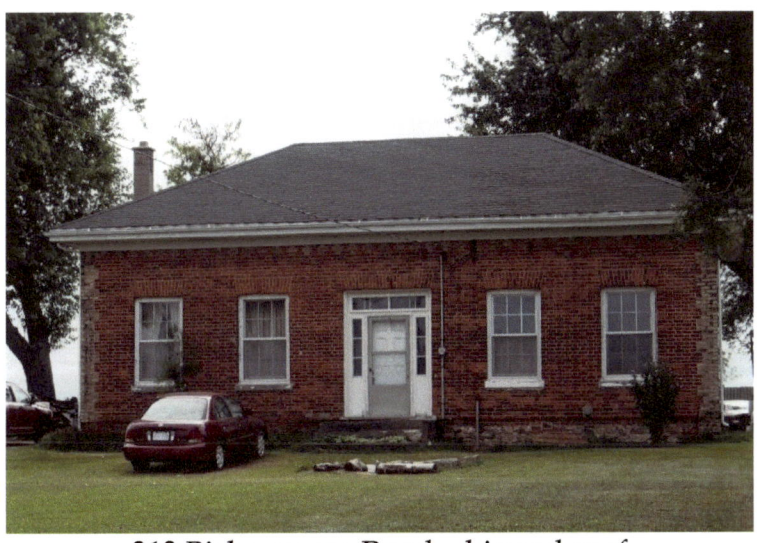

313 Bishopsgate Road – hipped roof

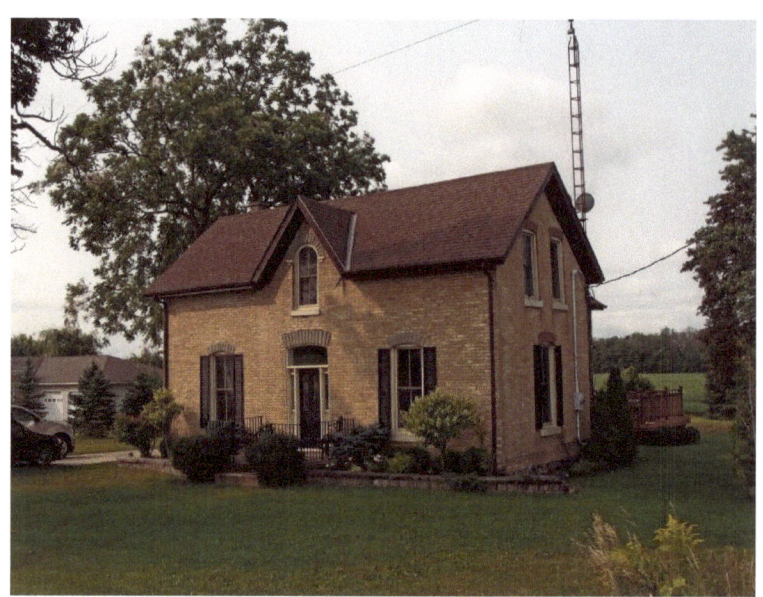

445 Bishopsgate Road - Gothic

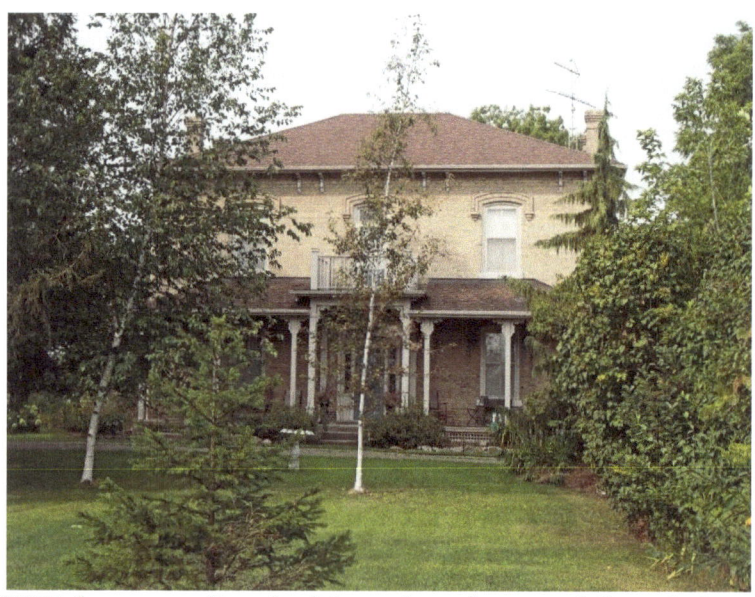

497 Bishopsgate Road – hipped roof, second floor balcony

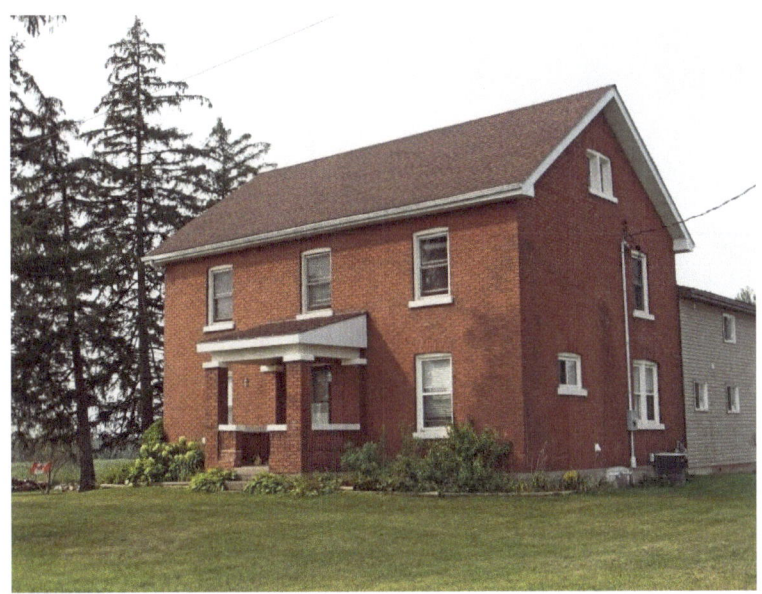

473 Bishopsgate Road – Many homes on this road are built of red brick. There was a brickyard operated by Richard Andrews in the early 1850s north of Bishopsgate Road, with perhaps another brickyard south of this road.

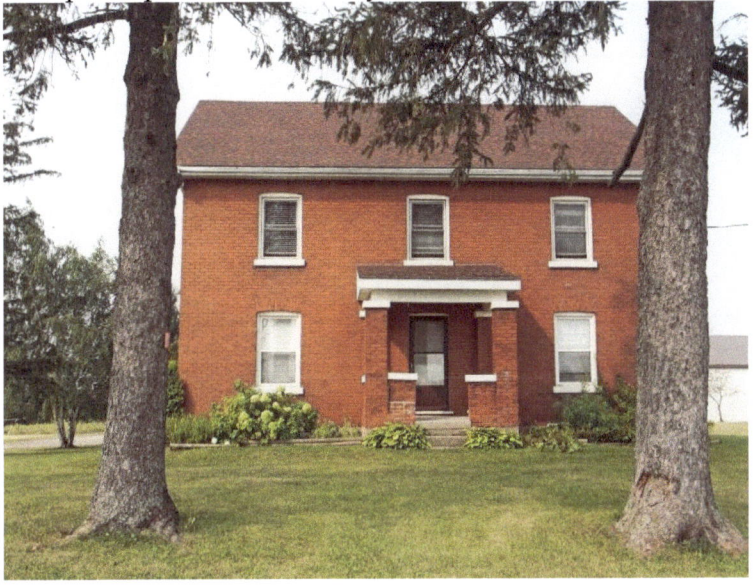

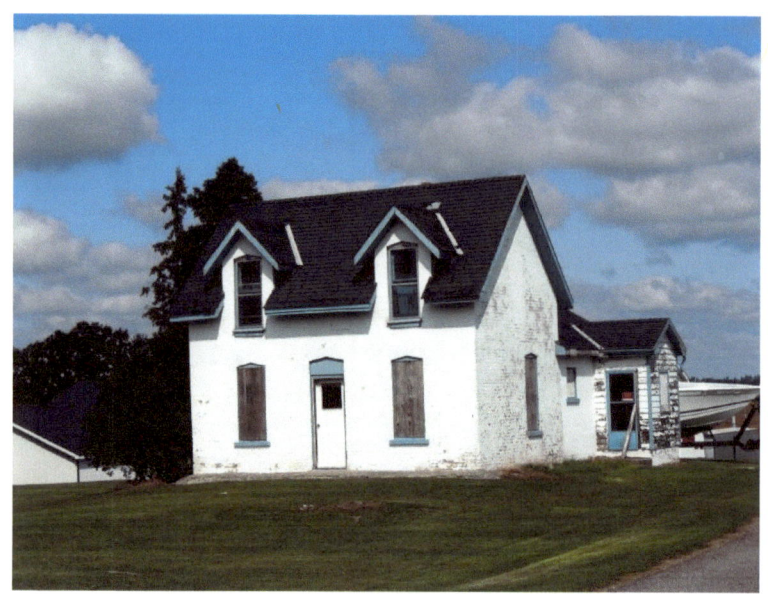

#1035

Mount Vernon

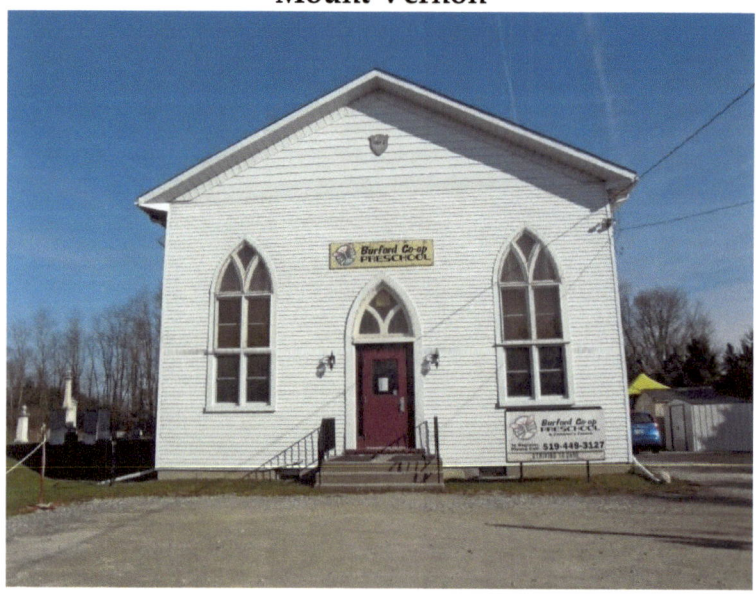

Mount Vernon Church - c. 1850 – Gothic style

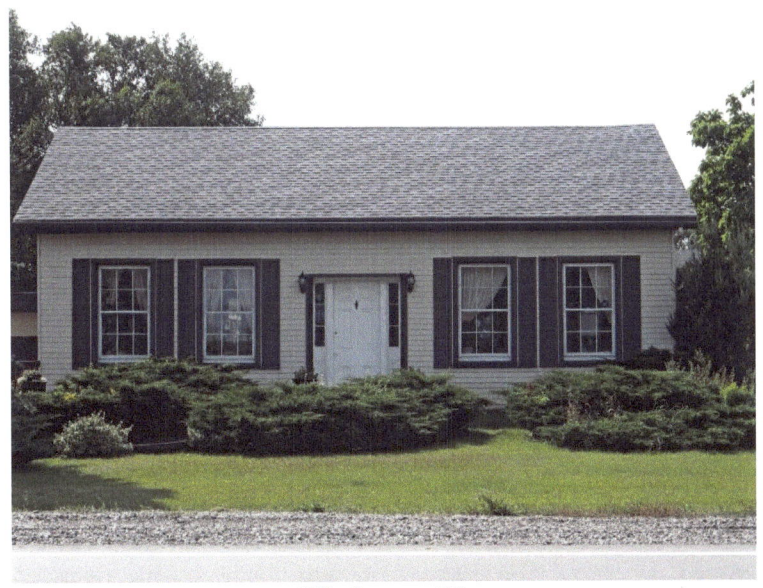

Highway 53

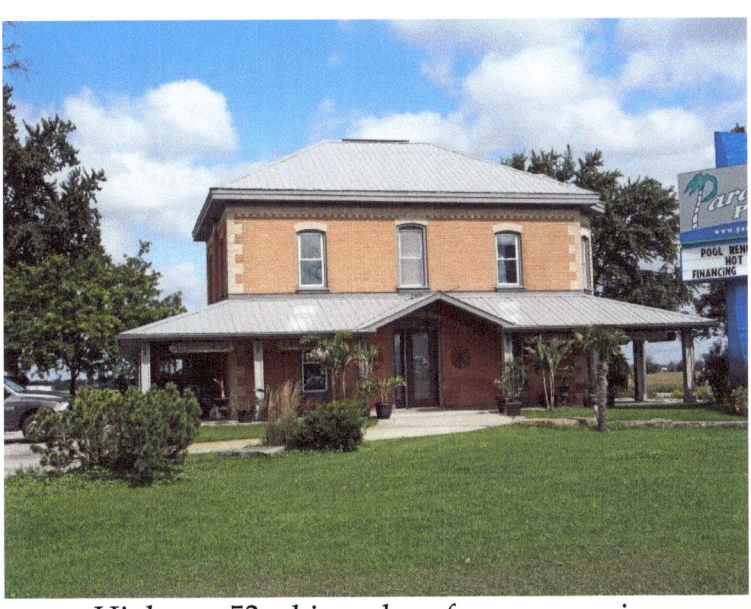

Highway 53 – hipped roof, corner quoins

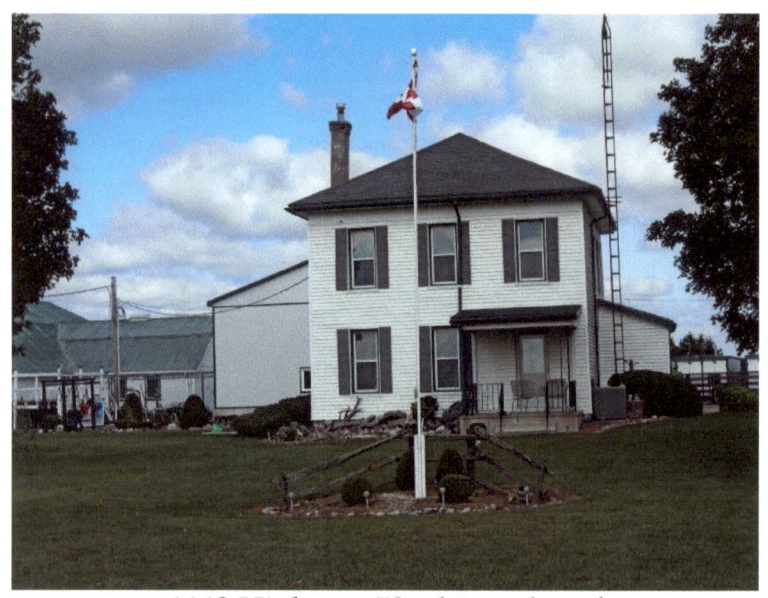

1149 Highway 53 – hipped roof

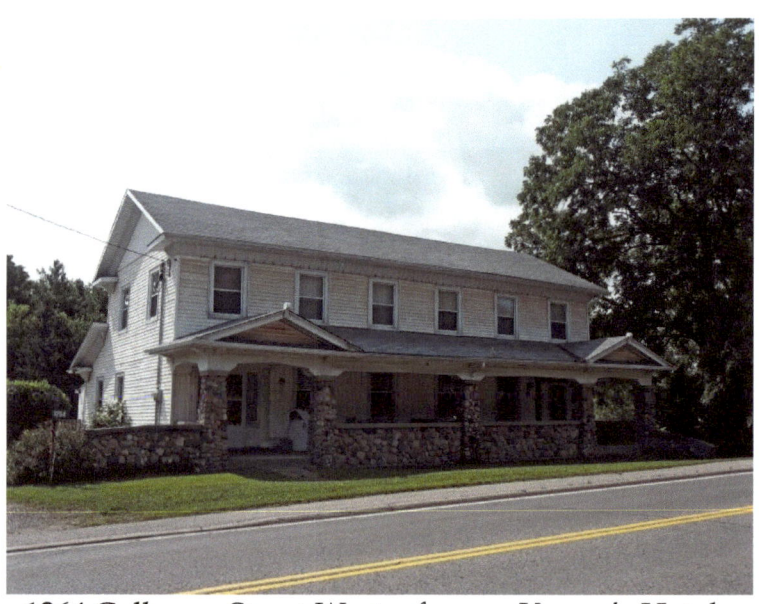

1264 Colborne Street West – former Kenny's Hotel - pediments

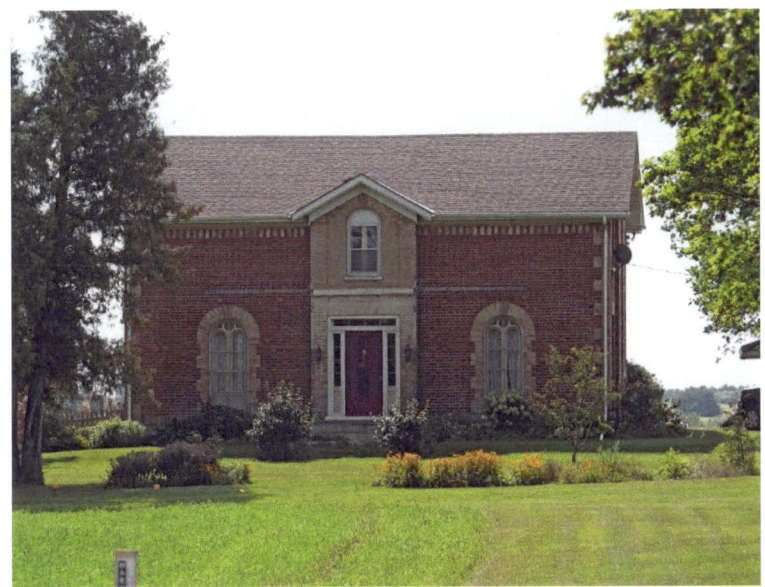

Colborne Street West – dentil molding under eaves, two-storey frontispiece, quoining on corners and around windows, sidelights and transom window

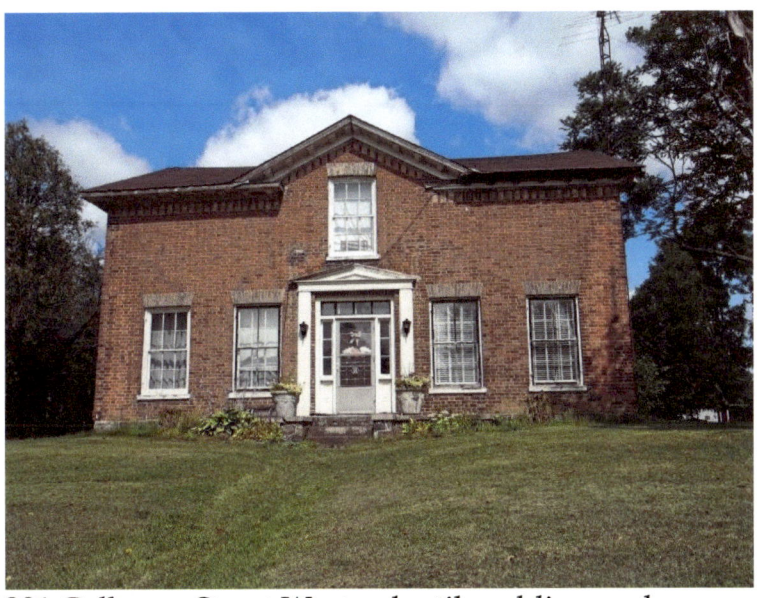

1291 Colborne Street West – dentil molding under eaves, sidelights and transom window

Bishopsgate

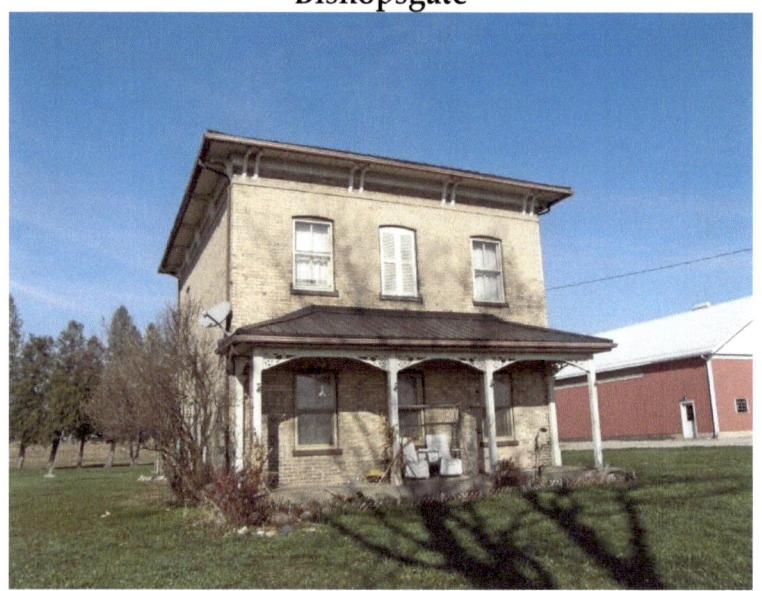

Paired cornice brackets

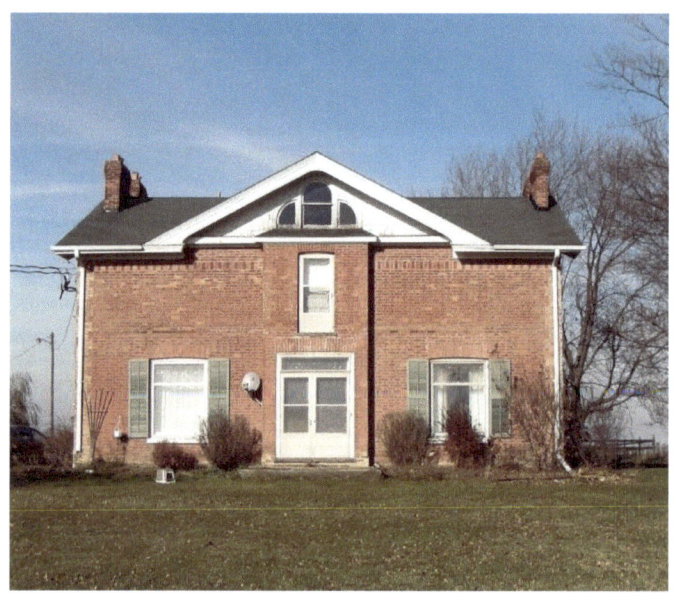

Langford

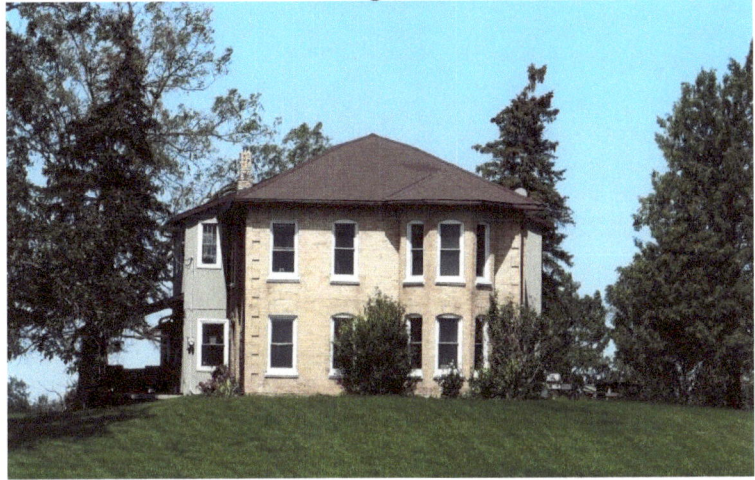

1700 Colborne Street East – hipped roof

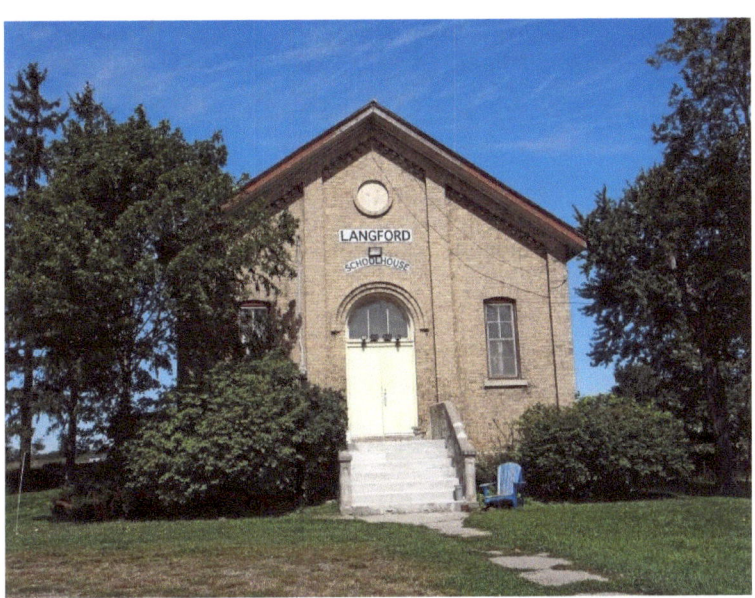

1694 Colborne Street East – Langford School – 1886 – Classical Revival style with elliptical arches over the windows and a rounded arch over the door. In 1964 the school closed and became a community hall. In 1988 the Jerseyville-Langford Nursery School began operating here.

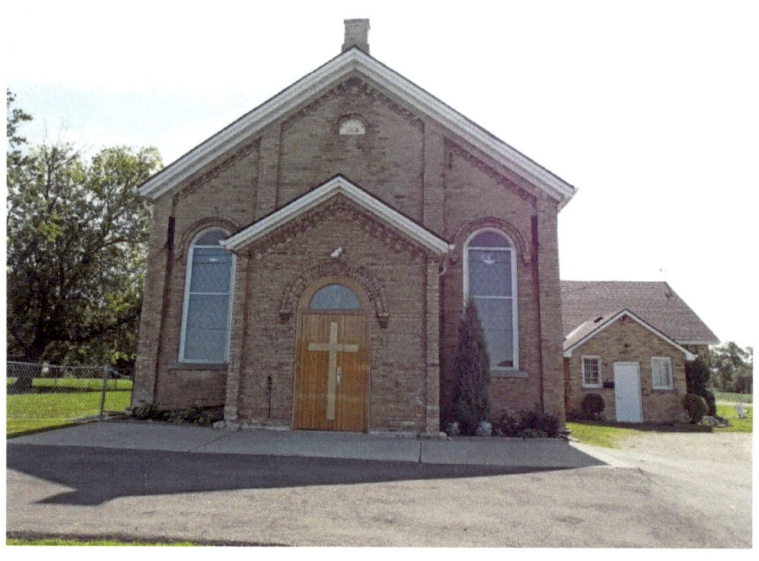

Langford Community Church – 1868 – at the corner of Highway 2/53 was first known as the Plank Road Church and later changed to the Langford Wesleyan Methodist Church. In 1925 it became Langford United Church and today it is Langford Community Church. The white brick church is in Classical Revival style with rounded arches above the windows and doors.

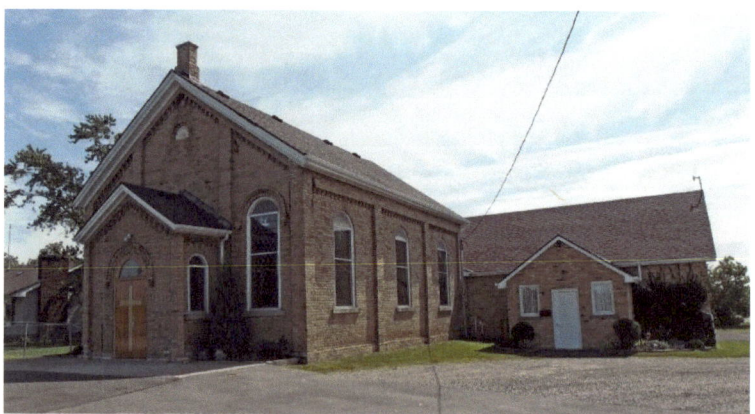

Burtch

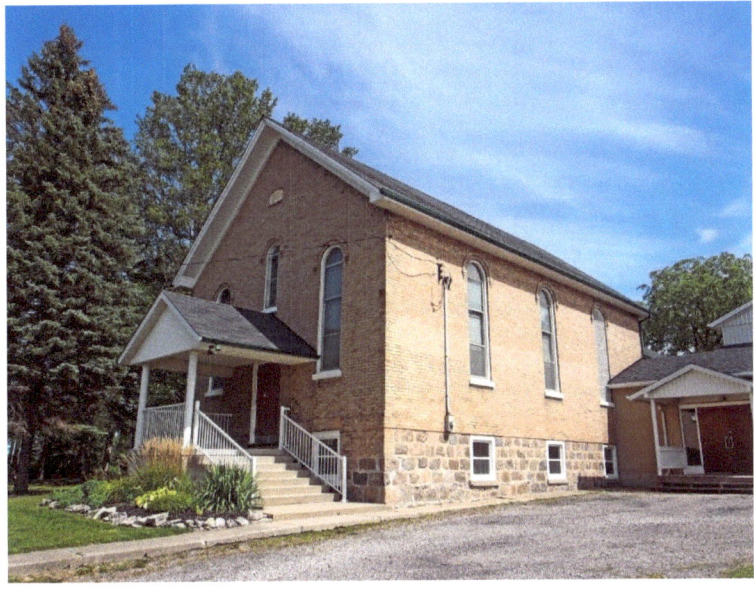

Burtch Baptist Church – Classical Revival style with rounded arches above the windows

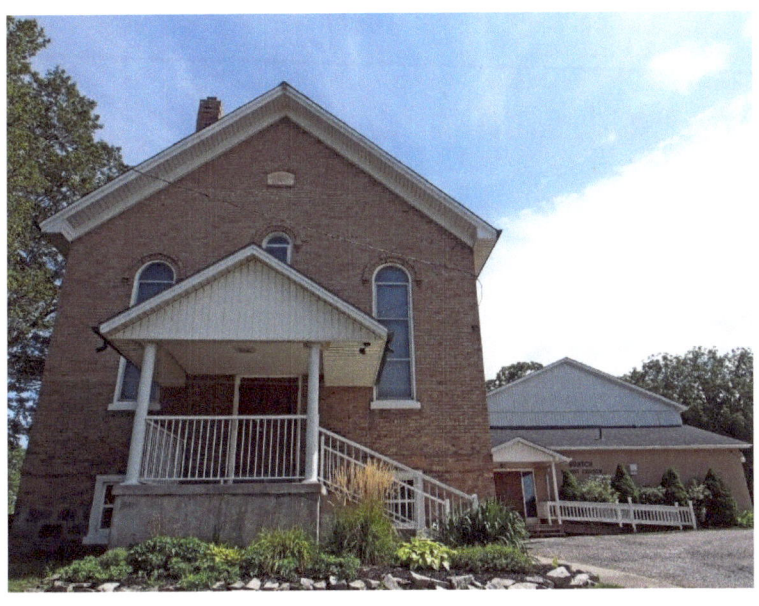

Architectural Terms

Bay Window: A window that projects out from a wall, in a semicircular, rectangular, or polygonal design. Used frequently in Gothic and Victorian designs. Example: 371 Maple Avenue South, Page 14	
Brackets: a decorative or weight-bearing structural element which forms a right angle with one side against a wall and the other under a projecting surface such as an eave or roof. Example: 358 Maple Avenue South, Page 12	
Cornice Return: decorative element on the end of a gable. Example: 363 Maple Avenue South, Page 13	
Dentil Moulding: an even series of rectangles used as ornamental decoration in cornices. Example: Colborne Street West, Page 37	
Dichromatic brickwork: the use of two colours of brick, tile or slate to decorate a façade. Example: 358 Maple Avenue South, Page 12	
Dormer: (French for "sleep") a gable end window that pierces through the plane of a sloping roof surface to create usable space in the top floor or attic of a building by adding headroom. Example: 381 Maple Avenue South, Page 16	

Fretwork: interlaced decorative design resembling a bracket Example: 270 Bishopsgate Road, Page 30	
Frontispiece: a portion of the façade of a building, usually a centred doorway that is slightly raised from the rest of the building, usually has extensive ornamentation. Frontispieces are usually Classical in design with white columned porches. Example: 401 Maple Avenue South, Page 21	
Gable: the triangular portion of a wall between the edges of a sloping roof. Example: 193 Bishopsgate Road, Page 27	
Hipped Roof: a roof where all sides slope downwards to the walls with no gables. Example: 84 Fairfield Road, Page 25	
Iron Cresting: A decorative ornament along the top of a roof. Iron cresting was popular in the Baroque era and also in Italianate, Victorian, Second Empire and Queen Anne styles of architecture. Example: 386 Maple Avenue South, Page 18	
Pediment: a triangular section above the door or portico, usually supported by columns. The inside of the triangle is called the tympanum. Example: 1264 Colborne Street West, Page 36	

Quoin: masonry blocks at the corner of a wall, often a decorative feature, usually larger or of a different colour than the rest of the wall. Example: 280 Maple Avenue South, Page 9	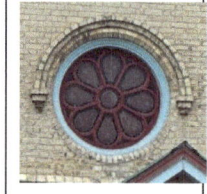
Rose Window: a circular window with ornamental tracery radiating from the centre. Example: 187 Maple Avenue South, Page 8	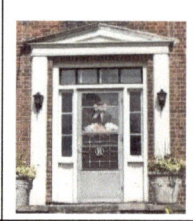
Sidelight: a vertical window that flanks a door, and is often used to emphasize the importance of a primary entrance. **Transom Window:** the light above the doorway, also called a fanlight. Example: 1291 Colborne Street West, Page 37	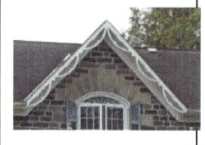
Verge board: also called bargeboards – hang from the projecting end of a roof and are often elaborately carved and ornamented. Example: 212 Bishopsgate Road, Page 27	

Building Styles

Classical Revival, 1820-1860 – This style was an analytical, scientific, and dogmatic revival based on intensive studies of Greek and Roman buildings, concerned with the application of Greek plans and proportions to civic buildings. Schools, libraries, government offices, and most other civic buildings were built in the Classical Revival style. The white columned porches of the Classical Revival domestic buildings are identified with the mansions of wealthy land owners in Canada. Example: Langford Community Church, Page 40	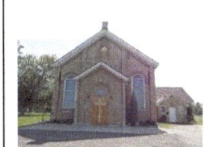
Georgian, before 1860 – This style began with the British King Georges in the 18th century. These buildings have balanced facades around a central door, medium-pitched gable roofs, and small paned windows. Example: 270 Bishopsgate Road, Page 30	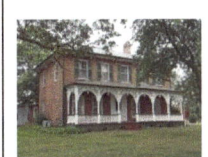
Gothic Revival, 1830-1890 – These decorative buildings have sharply-pitched gables with highly detailed verge boards, pointed-arch window openings, and dichromatic brickwork. It is a common style in Ontario. Example: 445 Bishopsgate Road, Page 32	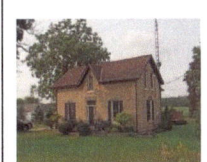

Italianate, 1850-1900 – A two story rectangular building with a mild hip roof, a projecting frontispiece, and generous eaves with ornate cornice brackets was the basis of the style; often there are large sash windows, quoins, ornate detailing on the windows, belvederes and wraparound verandahs. Italianate commercial buildings often have cast iron cresting and elegant window surrounds. Example: 358 Maple Avenue South, Page 12	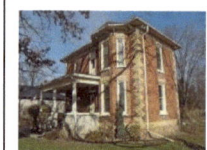
Neo-Classical, 1810-1850 – This style was a direct result of the War of 1812. Many Upper Canadians returning from the war with the United States were second or third generation Loyalists who had inherited land and means from their forefathers. Once the conflict had passed, they had the money and the time to expand their holdings and indulge their architectural whims. Both residential and commercial buildings were constructed on the traditional Georgian plan, but they had a new gaiety and light-heartedness. Detailing became more refined, delicate, and elegant. Example: 280 Maple Avenue South, Page 9	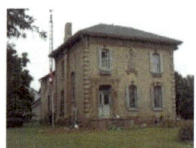

Ontario Cottage - one or one-and-a-half story buildings with a cottage or hip roof. The cottage roof is an equal hip roof where each hip extends to a point in the center of the roof. The hip roof has a long hip in the center. The Ontario Cottage is the vernacular design of the Regency Cottage which generally has a more ornate doorway and a partial or full verandah surrounding it. The roof can have a dormer, a belvedere, and generally two chimneys. Example: Maple Avenue South, Page 22	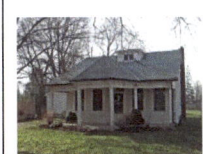
Queen Anne, 1885-1900 – This style is distinguished by an irregular outline featuring a combination of an offset tower, broad gables, projecting two-storey bays, verandahs, multi-sloped roofs, and tall, decorative chimneys. A mixture of brick and wood is common. Windows often have one large single-paned bottom sash and small panes in the upper sash. Example: 266 Bishopsgate Road, Page 30	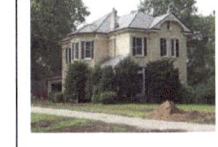

www.ingramcontent.com/pod-product-compliance
Lightning Source LLC
Chambersburg PA
CBHW040247220526
45473CB00001B/397